TABLE OF CONTENTS

T0347391

SUBSCRIBER INFORMATION

Educational Studies: A Journal of the American Educational Studies Association (ISSN 0013-1946) is published quarterly by Lawrence Erlbaum Associates, Inc., 10 Industrial Avenue, Mahwah, NJ 07430–2262. *Postmaster:* Send address changes to *Educational Studies,* 10 Industrial Avenue, Mahwah, NJ 07430–2262. Periodicals postage paid at Mahwah, NJ, and at additional mailing offices. Subscriptions for the 2002 volume are available on a calendar-year basis. In the United States and Canada, per-volume rates are US $35 for individuals and US $110 for institutions; in other countries, per-volume rates are US $65 for individuals and US $140 for institutions. Send subscription orders, information requests, and address changes to the Journal Subscription Department, Lawrence Erlbaum Associates, Inc., 10 Industrial Avenue, Mahwah, NJ 07430–2262. Address changes should include a copy of the mailing label. Claims for missing issues cannot be honored beyond 4 months after the mailing date. Duplicate copies cannot be sent to replace issues not delivered due to failure to notify publisher of change of address.

Electronic: Full-price print subscribers to Volume 33, 2002, are entitled to receive the electronic version free of charge. *Electronic-only* subscriptions are also available at a reduced price of $99.00 for institutions and $31.50 for individuals.

This journal is abstracted or indexed in *PsychINFO/Psychological Abstracts; Book Review Digest; Education Index/Abstracts; Sociological Abstracts;* EBSCOhost Products.

Microform copies of this journal are available through ProQuest Information and Learning, P. O. Box 1346, Ann Arbor, MI 48106–1346. For more information, call 1-800-521-0600, extension 2888.

ISBN: 978-0-8058-9622-0

EDITOR'S CORNER

When members of the Educational Studies Editorial Board expressed interest in putting together a Special Issue on 9/11 that we could have ready by Fall 2002, I was skeptical that we could pull it off. It wasn't from lack of interest that I balked but more from doubt that we could issue the Call for Papers, receive enough response, and get the submissions turned around in good time. Boy was I wrong.

The numbers of excellent manuscripts sent in so quickly after our call has stunned me. The biggest problem turned out to be not whether we would get enough response but how to make the crucial decisions as to which pieces to use. I thank all of the authors who sent us such heartfelt and thoughtful essays. I'm sorry that we didn't have the option of publishing them all.

The response is clearly a testimony to the intensity of this issue in all of our lives, and as such I shouldn't be surprised. The events of September 11, 2001, have touched, moved, shaken all of us both in ways we have been struggling to grapple with and ways we cannot even be aware of. Our teaching has been affected, our thinking has been affected, and our relationships have been affected. How not? I have been grateful to be part of this broad network of dedicated and compassionate people; to read such insightful, informative works; and to feel a sense of community that perhaps only such tragedy can bring to the fore.

I have also found myself both more intent and more doubtful about what I do. Does that make sense? I mean, I guess, that I feel less certain that we will have enough impact in time to stem what feels like a stampede of destructive human potential, and even more serious about taking on the challenge of tripping it up. I look to the Dalai Lama for help, and I also find myself yet again thanking the late Frank Hearn (my first sociology professor from Cortland State University) for getting me into all of this in the first place. I don't know where else I'd be happier spending my time, even though I sometimes think that I don't know a damn thing about what I should be doing.

Rather than going on about all that, I much prefer to turn these questions over to the voices in this issue to do what needs to be done. You will find a powerful article by Wendy Kohli that many of us heard her deliver as her American Educational Studies Association (AESA) presidential address in the fall of 2001, just weeks after this dreadful set of events. Asking us in her own wonderful, grounded, and insightful way to consider the inseparable mind, body, and spirit dimensions of our responsibilities as witnesses to and respondents to this horrible event, Wendy takes us with her on her own spiritual journey. And she reminds us, this way, that rational, predictable, disembodied responses simply will not do.

Alas, Maxine Greene's 2002 keynote address from AESA will not contribute to this issue, but her piece will be included in a later publication, along with a beautiful piece by Mary Bushnell about her work with Maxine at the Lincoln Center. However, another of Wendy's mentors, Bill Griffen, professor from her Cortland State days (Cortland is really quite a place!), analyzes the relationship of global corporate interests and the subsequent impact on the community of life that the war on terrorism brings to light. Mark Ginsburg and Nagwa Megahed give us a sweeping and in-depth lesson on the cultural and political contexts of the various countries involved and what we need to know to teach about these events in those contexts. And Donna Adair Breault gives a stirring account of the aesthetic power of poetry to help us reckon with our new world.

We have a powerful collection of reflective works by Jaylynne Hutchinson, Andrew McKnight, and Andi O'Conor on what they as Social Foundations professors and their students went through in the aftermath of the attacks, how their courses have both contributed to their students' (and their own) abilities to understand this current context, and how these courses have been reshaped. Christopher Knaus contributes poetry and Gene Provenzo his "Time Exposure." Both are insightful and creative pieces of work to help us think about what we are doing (and not doing) in the face of the ongoing events.

Indeed, we have all been changed by these events; the question is, of course, will it really make a difference? Will we wake up to the consumerist craze this country lives by? Will we recognize the ways all sorts of hierarchies—the same ones that brought the hijackers to this country to accomplish their violence—play into our daily decisions, beliefs, and behaviors? Will we stop to consider how other life-forms on this planet are being impacted by the bombs being dropped on Afghanistan? Or, what any of that means for the larger community that lives there? As Bill Griffen says, "Let us hope so."

Okay, enough from me; it's been a long couple of semesters and I'm afraid I'm feeling too cynical to write anything useful this morning. Although we have forgone Book Reviews in this issue, you will find much that is wise and useful in the essays that follow. I leave you to them and wish you all the best as we make our way through this difficult and intense time. And please (if there is some form of intelligence that hears such pleas), I say, bring on the daffodils and the redbuds! That's the best remedy for cynicism I can think of, and I am ready for that!

Respectfully,
Rebecca A. Martusewicz
Editor

ARTICLES

2001 American Educational Studies
Presidential Address
Situated Knowing: Mind, Body, and Soul

WENDY KOHLI
Fairfield University

This article situates the speaker as an embodied, traumatized witness to the
World Trade Center attack on 9/11. She incorporates her work as a feminist
philosopher of education to show the limits of our critical rational traditions
for understanding the effects of this profound experience.

My Disrupted Situation

For months I had difficulty focusing on a theme for my talk.[1] As the president of
this organization, was I supposed to speak directly about our field and the challenges we face? I think here, for example, of the arguments over
disciplinarity/interdisciplinarity; over what counts as "rigorous research"; over the
culture wars within. Or, as a scholar, was it my responsibility to share with you my
most current work as a philosopher of education? Or, as the director of a progressive urban teacher education program, was I obligated to talk about the contradictions and complexities of the theory–practice conundrum? Or, somehow, miracu-
lously, bring them all together?

The calendar became my nemesis as the summer evaporated and the date for
this conference approached all too quickly. One sitting would take me down one
path; the next day I'd scrap that idea and move on to another. I knew I wanted to sit-
uate myself/my body/my voice in this talk without being too autobiographical, too
personal. And I wanted to demonstrate my critical analytic skills without being too
abstract, too removed.

I attributed my inability to focus on the daily stress and distractions of my administrative job at The New School. But my struggle had much more to do with the
larger existential questions I've been facing since turning fifty last year: How
meaningful was the life I had chosen? What values and commitments did I want to
shape the *next* fifty years of my life? What difference was I making in the world?

And then Tuesday morning, September 11, came. As I looked out of the window of my beautiful new ninth-floor office on Twelfth Street in Greenwich Village, I saw first one, then two towers burn and crumble before my own eyes. Incredible. Literally unbelievable. Surreal. As all too many people felt, "just like out of a movie." Except this *was real,* all too real. Real people crashing, crushing to their deaths by the thousands, as others ran for their lives. Luckily I was blessed with no personal loss; just the vivid memories of a city in shock—of hundreds of glazed-eyed, ash-covered refugees finding their way home with me on the ferry across the Hudson to New Jersey.

The next day I awoke to what Alex Chadwick on National Public Radio's *Morning Edition* was describing as "a world we didn't imagine yesterday, to a different country." *Are* we in a different country? One that we didn't (or couldn't) imagine? What were/are the limits of our imagination, both individual and social? How are we intellectuals and teachers to respond to this incredible event? What and whose explanations can we count on? Can we rely on our taken-for-granted frameworks? What else is needed to make sense of the transformed world in which we now find ourselves? How are "we" to relate to the "they" in the rest of the world? Who is "us" and who is "them"? What is it going to require of all of us to be-in-the-world, together, in peace? These are the questions and impulses that shape this talk, that inform my life.

Responding to Our Newly Transformed World

The Red, White, and Blue

In moments of national tragedy, people often resort to clichés and myths for temporary comfort. The flag is wrapped and flown to demonstrate solidarity and loyalty. Even I found myself longing for the safety and certainty I remember as a child growing up in small-town America—baton twirling in Fourth of July parades with red, white, and blue streamers—or crying when singing the national anthem. Fact or fiction, I now find myself yearning for that state of childhood innocence.

At the same time, the critical educator in me (or is it my inner cynic?) worries about the emotional, nostalgic response surrounding me. In this univocal patriotic rush, to voice dissent feels tantamount to treason. Even at The New School, a place founded by pacifists in protest of the loyalty oath at Columbia University during World War I, the flag was flown on September 12. Most of us didn't even know The New School *owned* a flag! Some of us wondered aloud, "Who made the decision to fly it?" What and whose sentiments were being displayed? What meaning(s) are being read into that banner—from within the institution and from without? Does it matter?

All over New York City the flag was out in full color. Even Todd Gitlin, cultural critic and Vietnam War-era peace activist, explained his decision to fly the flag. In his defense, he insisted on *multiple readings* of the gesture, expressing solidarity with the victims of the attack, not just endorsing general patriotic fervor. Possible?

Yes ... and no.... Certainly it is possible both to insist on multiple readings of a cultural icon like the flag and to resist the patriotic lockstep; but with the rhetoric circulating from Washington and New York—centers of political and cultural power—one must fight hard to make room for alternatives.

Did you notice? Even the NBC Peacock gave up her rainbow-colored plumage for the red, white, and blue of Old Glory. And school boards all over the country—including New York City—are going back to pre-Vietnam recitation of the pledge of allegiance as a sign of patriotic solidarity. I, and I am sure many of you, would like to keep the dialogue open, the door ajar, to allow for multiple perspectives to be heard, to ensure that we do not have to go back to the "love it or leave it" days of the sixties. It is possible to be both against the massive bombing of Afghanistan and for some retaliatory measures against bin Laden and the Taliban.

Personal Witnessing, Subjective Experience, and the Problematic of Categorization

As the tragedy unfolded, personal stories were told and retold in an attempt to grasp, in their cumulative particularity, the enormity of the situation. Even I, for days, needed to rehearse my experience on that fateful day, even though I wasn't *really* at risk. Shrines emerged on the city streets—Union Square, Washington Square Park, Grand Central Terminal, neighborhood fire stations—surrounded by photographs and descriptions of lost loved ones. Personal obituaries began appearing in the *New York Times,* with the commitment to each and every one of the nearly 5,000[2] people killed on the four airplanes, at the Pentagon, and in the World Trade Center. Vignettes appeared—recounting the specialness of a father, the determination of a daughter, the sweetness of a mother, the success of a son, the bravery of a cop—putting faces, personal narrative, lived experience on the abstract, distancing statistics. This *subjectification,* this refusal to *reduce to objects* the "victims" of the attacks, challenges our tendency to categorize, to generalize, and to think in either/or terms. Even the New York Police Department is no longer seen so coldly by its critics. The category has become more fluid, perhaps more *real?*

Audre Lorde comes to mind in her now classic *Sister Outsider* where she says,

> Much of Western European history conditions us to see human differences in simplistic opposition to each other: dominant/subordinate, good/bad, superior/inferior. In a society where the good is defined in terms of profit rather than in terms of human need, there must always be some group of people, who, through systematized oppression, can be made to feel surplus, to occupy the place of the dehumanized inferior. (Lorde 1984, 114)

The prevailing belief in recent years was that New York City police positioned people of color as inferior, as ripe for profiling and even shooting. And the cops, in turn, were positioned as racist. The particularities, the subjective accounts of the bravery of the NYPD during this crisis, disrupted that categorical imperative—as have the responses to the NYPD by communities of color. Six months ago it would have been unimaginable to see people of color wearing NYPD baseball caps. But now we see people on all sides of the brutality issue allowing for more generous renderings of each other. Short-lived? Perhaps, but at least it's an opening.

Edward Said is another scholar who speaks against the problematic and persistent tendencies toward labels, toward dualisms. Concerned not so much with the "victims" and the "heroes" of the WTC attack, he, in a recent article in *The Nation,* attends to the "perpetrators" of the heinous crime and how they are positioned in the discourse of "the clash of civilizations." He says,

> How finally inadequate are the labels, generalizations, and cultural assertions. At some level, for instance, primitive passions and sophisticated know-how converge in ways that give the lie to a fortified boundary not only between "West" and "Islam" but also between past and present, us and them, to say nothing of the very concepts of identity and nationality about which there is unending disagreement and debate. (Said 2001, 12)

I myself must confess to some guilt in this area of categorization and labels. I live in Hoboken, New Jersey—the mile-long city known as the hometown of Frank Sinatra, the dockside inspiration for *On The Waterfront,* and the (contested) birthplace of baseball. It is a city of immigrants—Italian, Portuguese, Puerto Rican, Cuban, Irish, German—and more recently, Yuppies. Young whippersnappers with lucrative jobs in the hot stock market were responsible, along with the real estate developers and corrupt local politicians, for the gentrification of the city since the eighties. When my husband, Philip, and I moved here two years ago, we felt out of place, out of time. Conversations overheard on the bus to the PATH station confirmed our stereotypes: new rich, on paper at least, who had more money in their stock portfolios from two years of working on Wall Street, than we had for our retirement after twenty years of professional life. Not the conditions for friend making. Too many boundaries to cross, too many prejudices to defeat, too many labels to peel off.

When we bought our condo, we inherited neighbors below us—three young men—who worked in stocks and bonds. Every morning I'd see three—not one, but three!—*Wall Street Journals* on the front stoop awaiting them. We had and made little contact, except for an occasional hello in passing, or an infrequent phone call on the weekends to quiet their alcohol-induced partying. I objectified them and, in doing so, dehumanized them. In Lorde's terms, I constructed them as *inferior* to me.

Then came September 11. I can say that when I finally reached the safety and comfort of my own home on that horrific day, I felt genuine concern and compassion for those three guys. I wanted to make sure they made it home alive, and I wanted to make a human connection with them. Naiveté? I don't think so. I learned that, at least in those first traumatic moments, they, too, saw me in a new light. The categories softened, the judgments melted away, allowing us to communicate in a more respectful, individuated way.

Another category was dislodged in the aftermath of the WTC attack: that of Bob Kerrey as "war criminal." Kerrey is now the president of New School University—my "commander in chief," if you will. Soon after he was installed last February, the news broke in *The New York Times Magazine* and on CBS with Dan Rather that Kerrey had led an assault on civilians in Vietnam when he was a young lieutenant. His memory of this incident—some would call it an atrocity—is slippery. And his apparent refusal, at least in his public remarks, to understand it now in more expanded terms than his own self-healing process, made me a bit skeptical of him overall. But I couldn't actually utter the words "war criminal" when describing him, although I understood how others could. One reason for that was that I had already had regular personal contact with him, conferring with him about the New School's commitment to NYC public schools. That personal, experiential knowledge made it more difficult for me to categorize him, objectify him, judge him, dismiss him.

After September 11, it became even more complicated. Kerrey called a meeting of the university community on Thursday, September 13. He very forcefully encouraged us, especially us at The New School, with its political legacy, to provide an alternative voice to the warpath that Bush was hawking. Kerrey spoke movingly in several contexts about how the war metaphor was doomed; that the history of American foreign policy and actions in the region had contributed to the attack. He spoke courageously, taking stands and asking us to create the intellectual and moral climate to do the same. He also spoke of the physical courage required to go against the grain at this time of local and national suffering. I was struck by his references to courage: physical, moral, ethical, intellectual courage. It *does* take courage to think for oneself, to act for oneself, to disagree with one's peers, family, or boss. Maybe he had, after all, learned from his dastardly deed as a Navy SEAL. Now, as a leader of a relatively progressive university, with some amount of cultural capital and political influence, he was encouraging us, as individuals and as a community, to take action and speak out. This stance doesn't erase his past record, nor does it lead me to give up my own critical intelligence, but it does remind me of the contradictions and human failures we all inhabit, to one degree or another.

Education, the Emotions, and the Need for Heteroglossia

Emotional responses to the WTC attack here in the United States have ranged from utter numbness to profound sadness to gut-wrenching fear to retaliatory anger, and are changing the more time elapses. Some commentators employed critical analysis to understand the complexities of what happened, but most in the mainstream media stayed with the mere descriptive, banal, or even shamelessly patriotic—witness the Dan Rather interview where he made his emotional pledge to follow President Bush, our commander in chief, wherever he asked him to go. And "good citizens" were implored to remain "united" behind the president and his policies, regardless of one's own deeply held political and moral commitments.

It didn't take long for me to wonder what impact this catastrophe would have on my own work as a critical educator and scholar-citizen. How would I integrate this experience into the "curriculum" of future teachers and counter the reactionary voices like Lynne Cheney and Chester Finn who were using this terrible national tragedy as another opportunity to attack multiculturalism and promote the hegemony of American culture and history?

What lessons was I to learn from all of this? How has this trauma affected the landscapes of my psyche, the contours of my imagination, the possibilities (or impossibilities) for pedagogical and political action? What do my students need and want from all of this? Should I respond to their emotional trauma—or is that out-of-bounds? Am I professionally obligated to "keep to the content"? Or do extraordinary circumstances require extraordinary boundaries? *Is it a different world?* If so, in what ways? If not, will I—we—soon return to business as usual? If so, what will that business look like?

Just the fact that these questions have emerged for me is testimony to how deeply entrenched is the bifurcation between mind/emotion. "We" intellectuals are assumed to be ill equipped to deal with "the emotions." Out of fear that we are incompetent, out of "reasoned" judgment of our own limitations, we disqualify ourselves from this arena. We say, "Let the counselors and student services people handle 'that part' of the students' lives; we are here to teach history, or philosophy, or mathematics." As if our students come to us *with only their heads;* or as if *we* come to them *with only our* heads.

Working only a few blocks from Ground Zero and living right across the river from lower Manhattan, I am able to experience with all my senses the graphic scope of this disaster—the sights, the sounds, the smells, the feel of a traumatized city. This witnessed trauma is now inscribed on/in me—my body, my mind, and my psyche. And every time I revisit the trauma, I somatasize.

Just one week after the attack, our dean invited a military analyst and expert on terrorism to speak to our regular monthly Chairs and Directors meeting. This apparently decent guy from Northern Ireland, well trained in his narrow, technical field, proceeded to tell us, "Your life as you know it is going to change forever ... for the rest of your lives, you will now have to contend with the uncertain certainty of terrorist activity, just like the rest of the world. America and Americans are no longer immune." We have lost our innocence and our privileged quietude.

The more he spoke, the tighter my stomach got and the sicker I felt. My body was saying, "Enough! Don't tell me any more details about how I am going to be attacked by anthrax or a suitcase nuclear device." I *embodied* the terror and the powerlessness—even rage—that I felt in response to his analysis and to the general situation in which I was placed. Later that night, in a state of insomnia, my anxiety got the best of me, and I woke my husband to tell him we should move to the Adirondacks, that NYC was no longer a safe place for us to live and work. My stomach continued to guide my thinking. Was this "reasonable"? I don't know; it certainly *felt* reasonable. But what does this mean? Isn't *feeling* reasonable an oxymoron? How does this traumatized situation affect my knowing, my understanding of the world and my action in it? To what degree should I trust my gut responses?

I take to heart the powerful insights Deborah Britzman offers about "education as psychic event" (Britzman 1998, 3). In her return to and re-visioning of Freudian psychoanalysis, she pushes us who toil in the vineyards of educational studies to consider the limits of our critical paradigms. Britzman maintains that even though those frameworks have led to honorable practices like antiracist pedagogy, they still assume that "learning proceeds by way of direct apprehension, that experience is always conscious experience, and that identity organizes political consciousness" (4). For Britzman, this approach, although well intended, is not adequate to the task: "yet another history must be admitted: that of the unconscious" (5).

Although I am not pursuing a psychoanalytic analysis of education in this talk, I do agree that our received framework of critical rationality is inadequate to understand the layers of lived human experience or the formation of one's ethical stance. I, like Maxine Greene, want to argue for Bakhtin's heteroglossia of voices, in order "to enlarge one's experience with multiplicity of perspectives" (Greene 1988, 129). This will require us to rethink our criteria of what counts as good scholarship, since not only do we categorize in either/or ways, but *we make judgments* as we do it: It's either a good theory or one to be rebutted entirely. We rarely embrace a both/and stance in how we come to understand the world.

I would like to suggest that a healthy dialogue across different theoretical frameworks adds greatly to one's understanding(s) of complex subjects. I invoke Greene again: "many have been engaging in what Mikhail Bakhtin called 'dialogism,' viewing literary texts as spaces where multiple voices and multiple discourses intersect and interact" (1988, 129). No *one* frame can grasp adequately the multiple dimensions and experiences of a situation. One need not give up one's critical capacities to embrace differing, perhaps even contradictory, theories. I think here of what I learned from Hans Georg Gadamer when doing my dissertation two decades ago (Kohli 1984). He argued that, contrary to the critical theory of Jurgen Habermas, a hermeneutical approach to understanding (where one incorporated *multiple horizons*—multiple perspectives) provided an inherently *critical* capacity for understanding. Habermas would insist that it, necessarily, led one down the slippery slope of radical relativism. For Gadamer, one needs to be in dialogue with a *range* of perspectives, *from within one's own situatedness,* to come to a fuller, more plausible understanding of the world.

This persuasion influenced how I, in later years, constructed a reader in philosophy of education (Kohli 1995). In order to contribute to this volume, authors were required to engage each other in a dialogical format across their differences. This entailed a commitment to a "good faith effort to resist 'going for the jugular,' to avoid immediately 'finding the flaw in the argument,' to overcome their training in philosophy to 'get it right'" (Kohli 1995, xiv). I believed then, as I do now, that this open, engaging, dialogical stance would not require contributors to give up their integrity or to abandon their standards of critical reflection. On the contrary, it would allow for teaching and learning to take place, for us to listen and see new possibilities. It was a way to move out of either/or thinking; to admit to the incompleteness of knowledge, to the limits of knowing from our own situatedness.

A multivalent frame needs to be deployed in order for me to answer the questions: What have I learned from the immediacy of experience of this terrible attack on my beloved city? And what courage do I need in order to muster a response—even a range of responses—to the lessons learned, to the trauma I've inherited, to what Britzman might call a kind of "difficult knowledge" (19)? A clear, rational understanding, for example, of the historical reasons for the current crisis will no longer satisfy. That may be necessary perhaps, but not sufficient. We need to complement, even transform our privileging of a particular kind of rationality, of a particular kind of knowing. We need to have the courage to incorporate psychological insights, *bodily* knowledge, and even *spiritual* transformation into our critical analysis.

Bodily Knowing

Maxine Greene (1995), our teacher, colleague, and friend, reminds us that

> We are first cast into the world as embodied beings trying to understand. From particular situated locations, we open ourselves to fields of perception. Doing so, we begin to inhabit varied and always incomplete multiverses of forms, contours, structures, colors and shadows. We become present to them as consciousness in the midst of them, not as outside observers; and so we see aspects and profiles but never totalities. We reach into the world—touching, listening, watching what presents itself to us from our own prereflective landscapes, primordial landscapes. (73)

Greene, with her roots in existential phenomenology, has written for three decades from a situated space. Challenging one of the main tenets of analytic philosophy, a philosophic approach that pretends a "view from nowhere," Greene can be seen as the precursor to many contemporary feminist theorists who now take for granted attention to context and body. Influenced by Merleau-Ponty, among others, Greene (1973) saw that he had something important to say to us about early learning in the context of a primary reality. She maintains that

> For Merleau-Ponty, this original world is the natural and social domain in which the individual as child was first involved *corporeally and affectively.* Touching, smelling, listening, crawling about his [sic] physical environment, the child be-

came aware of his surroundings before he was capable of logical or predictive thought. He perceived what lay around him; and perceiving, he organized his world around his *body,* around himself. (emphasis added; 1973, 160–161)

I want to encourage a dialogue here on what it would mean for us as educational theorists to incorporate corporeality and affect into our analysis of education and schooling, into our theories of teaching and learning. I want us to think about what it would mean to decenter the mind/body split, to center the body as well as the mind.

My own intellectual training, rooted squarely in the rational discourse of the Frankfurt School, made venturing into this expanded domain challenging. Nevertheless, my grasp of lived experience made it equally *impossible* to deny other frameworks for understanding. I can no longer ignore the insights coming from scholars I respect. Significant ramifications result for education and curriculum, it seems to me, with a rethinking of the body (and mind), given how implicated educational theory and practice is in the body's erasure through the privileging of "mind over matter."

Body Talk

The body—the "lived" body, the "material" body, the "inscribed" body, the "disciplined" body, the "abject" body, the "medicalized" body, the "performed" body, the "historicized" body, the "trangressive" body—is now fashionable. The body is *in.* New theorizing (a)bounds across disciplinary boundaries in an effort to deconstruct the received views of corporeality. Drawing primarily on French feminism, poststructuralism, and psychoanalysis, a host of authors is placing the body at the center of its analyses of subjectivity, identity, and power.[3] Feminist philosophers have deconstructed the "legacy of rationality and how it has shaped and continues to influence conceptions of society … and knowledge"(Harvey and Okruhlik 1992, xi). Genevieve Lloyd (1989) is one who reminds us of our powerful Cartesian inheritance when she says, "the search for the 'clear and distinct,' [involves] the separating out of the emotional, the sensuous, the imaginative" (116).

This separating, this shedding of the corporeal, requires a particular kind of training. Men, for example, had to *learn* to be rational; they had to be *trained* out of their soft emotions and their sensuousness (Lloyd 1989, 116–117). This training is, of course, what Foucault called disciplining, which takes place at the site of the body. One pertinent, rather extreme, example of this may be seen in the way certain young Afghan boys under the Taliban regime were reportedly trained to fight, to have contempt for women, to live removed from the contamination of women. Of course, one could argue that all military regimes discipline their men to be antiemotion, antisex, antifemale to some degree or another.

Susan Bordo (1989) asserts that "the body is not only a text of culture … it is also a *practical,* direct locus of social control" (13). She puts it well: "Our conscious politics, social commitments, striving for change may be undermined and betrayed by the life of our bodies—not the craving, instinctual body imagined by Plato, Augustine and Freud but the *docile, regulated body* practiced and habituated to the rules of cultural life" (13).

Liz Grosz (1994) is another feminist theorist who seeks to re-dress the disciplining effects of the "regime of reason," a regime that produces the separation of mind from body. She suggests that many philosophers, including some feminists, "have tended to ignore the body or to place it in the position of being somehow subordinate to or dependent for all that is interesting about it ..." (vi). By inverting centuries of philosophical canon, Grosz works against the body's erasure and insists that "bodies have all the explanatory power of minds" (vii). She would concur with Maxine Greene that Merleau-Ponty was one philosopher who did not ignore the body. As Grosz tells it, he "begins with a fundamental presumption, not of Cartesian dualism of mind and body but of their necessary interrelatedness" and posits "the negative claim that the body is not an object. It is the condition and context through which I am able to have a relation to objects" (86).

Iris Young (1990) echoes this when she says, "in asking how there can be a world for a subject, Merleau-Ponty reorients the entire tradition of that questioning by locating a subjectivity not in mind or consciousness, but in the *body*" (147). She argues that he "gives to the lived body the ontological status that Sartre ... attribute[d] to consciousness alone" (147). Yet, Grosz cautions us to be wary of relying on [male] phenomenological accounts of the body, accounts that "[are] unable to address—the question of sexual difference, the question of *what* kind of *human body*" [emphasis added] is under discussion (1994, 110). According to Grosz, Merleau-Ponty "never once in his writings [makes] any suggestion that his formulations may have derived from the valorization and analysis of the experiences of only one kind of subject"—the male subject (110).

The same concern can be raised about Foucault. Although Foucault's genealogical work on disciplinary normalization offers feminists useful insight into power as constitutive, not simply repressive, and provides understandings of how pleasure and desire are produced, "he rarely discusses *female* bodies and pleasures, let alone *women's sex and desires*" (Grosz 1994, 156). One can only wonder, as Grosz does, that "in lieu of any specification, one must presume ... that the *neutral body* can only be unambiguously filled in by the *male body and men's pleasures* [emphasis added]" (156).

Sex, Desire, and the Education of the Body

Sex, desire. Sexual desire. These are subjects, like emotions in general, that usually fall outside the boundaries of educational discourse. They are also subjects that most teachers are not allowed to speak about with their students, except in the most clinical of ways. We are trained not to think of our colleagues or our students in sexual terms—for good reason perhaps—since we live in a society with such confused and contradictory views about sex and sexuality. However, just because something is difficult, complex, even a bit *dangerous,* doesn't mean we should avoid it.

There are some courageous scholars, like Allison Jones, who have tackled this topic, opening up new lines of discourse. Jones, employing a poststructuralist frame, suggests that we look anew at sexual harassment in educational settings in order to understand the way desire circulates in the classroom. For Jones,

> The teacher and the student each desire and need the other; each seek pleasure from/in the other, through the work they do. ... As a result, pedagogical relationships are often riven with vulnerability and anxiety—as well as pleasure and excitement. (1996, 103)

I believe, as does Jones, that if we ignore sex, desire, and pleasure—if we sweep them under the rug—we do so at our peril. They will only return to haunt us in a repressed form. There are political, educational, social, and psychological consequences to this avoidance. In fact, some recent research suggests that in sex-negative societies, there is a tendency toward more violence in general, as well as more child abuse, more homophobia, more discrimination against women (DeMeo 1998, 4). And we know of the controversial, admittedly heteronormative work of A. S. Neill and Wilhelm Reich, who argued that sex-positive, nonauthoritarian environments for children were more likely to produce more gentle, sincere, cooperative people. James DeMeo reminds us of Reich's work on the authoritarian personality and that "sexual pathology and cruelty to children were primal sources of the fascist character structure and totalitarian state apparatus" (42). Granted, this research is speculative, problematic, and certainly arguable, but we *should* be arguing with it. We should be challenging it and developing new lines of inquiry, not pretending that it is irrelevant to our scholarly or pedagogical work.

Spiritual Knowing

Now I want to return for a moment to my introduction—to my desire for situated knowing, for a meaningful life. I want to dig deep inside for the courage to speak about matters that we academics, with all of our training and intellectualism, generally dismiss: *Spiritual* matters—matters of the heart, matters of love, matters of human connection, matters of emotional and spiritual transformation. For me to talk honestly about a meaningful, integrated, situated life, I have to acknowledge my own spiritual journey—and not relegate it to the margins. Not cover it with embarrassment. Not give in to the fear of identifying as a "believer," albeit a "rational" believer.

I realize that after September 11, it is trickier than ever to talk about anything related to religion, particularly in the secular domain. The threat of fundamentalism in all its forms—Jewish, Muslim, Hindu, Christian—keeps us at arms length from embracing "irrational" thoughts or systems of belief. Yet, I feel it is more important than ever to open this conversation since we have all been affected on multiple levels, in many dimensions of our lives. I want to be able to respond as someone who shuns monovocal interpretations, who invites heteroglossia, who struggles with and against essentialism.

A few years ago I became a Jew. In Conservative and Reform Judaism, this process is referred to as "choosing" to become a Jew, not "converting." It is seen as a "rational" choice, not due to some mystical moment of "seeing the light," or witnessing a burning bush, or hearing Moses speak to me from a mountain. It results from reading and reflection and arguing and analysis, as much as from a heartfelt desire to make meaning in my life.

Over time, I noticed my Judaism affecting my work. As a social activist, I have always made connections between my political work and my intellectual work, much to the dismay of some of my colleagues in Philosophy of Education who think the boundaries should be maintained firmly. I have sought out a radical *praxis,* an integration between my theoretical stance and my political and pedagogical practices. This parallels one of the main tenets of Judaism, *Tikkun Olam,* repairing the tears in the fabric of the universe—to work to make the world better in every dimension. For Jews, there is an ontological necessity to act in and on the world, in our lifetime; not wait until some hereafter to attain goodness. I see more clearly than ever the synchronicity between who I am as Jew and what I do as a scholar-teacher. I no longer choose to keep an artificial separation between those identities.

In sorting out this problematic terrain, I have been blessed with the support of progressive teachers and practitioners of Judaism—people who value the role the intellect can play in interpreting the world and who are committed to making the world better for all, not just for a chosen few. Some of these teachers are colleagues and members of AESA. Another is Michael Lerner, the founding editor of *Tikkun,* a progressive journal for Jewish thought.[4] Lerner has worked doggedly over the years to create the space for open debate among Jews on Israel and "the Palestinian situation." He has had the courage to speak out, and to encourage others to speak out, for the rights of Palestinians to a homeland, risking physical and psychological harassment, including death threats and monetary reprisals. Lerner also has worked with Cornel West to increase the dialogue between Blacks and Jews (Lerner and West 1995). In his recent book, *Spirit Matters* (2000, 3), Lerner even borrows from the title of West's (1993) book *Race Matters* to elaborate his theory about spirituality. It's to Lerner's work that I now turn to enlarge our conversation here. Like him, I want to include in this conversation both "those who look on spiritual transformation as a threat to rationality and humanism and those who see it as a hopeful development for the human family" (3). Writing before September 11, Lerner knew that many people [were turning] to the realm of Spirit to try to make sense of pain and suffering they've experienced. Others have sensed that there is something deeply missing in their lives and have found that the rewards of the marketplace don't satisfy their hunger for some framework of meaning and purpose in their lives. (3)

For Lerner, this "hunger for meaning and purpose is as strong and central to human life as the hunger for food or for sex" (10).

Clearly *after* September 11, these questions of meaning and purpose have come to the fore for many more of us. I know they have for me. Although never one to embrace the market—in fact, I've been a critic of capitalism since my college days—I still have been on my own kind of treadmill within the academic market. I've been upwardly mobile, implicated in, if not embracing of, the competitive trajectory of academia. I've participated in the careerist path of knowledge production, churning out articles for tenure and promotion, and assessing another's value on quantity as much as quality. I could defend myself and say that this is what the game is, and that to be in the game, I need to follow the rules or hurt myself. True ... yet not. Once tenured, there is no need to keep the rules going. Why not risk? What is there to lose?

Now I want to challenge myself to really live according to the complex, even contradictory values and beliefs important to me. To do so, I want to act on my *spiritual* knowing, as much as I act on my rational and bodily knowing.[5] I am not talking about organized religion here, nor am I proselytizing to convert others to my cause. I do, however, want to name something that is important to me in how I come to my work, to my teaching, to my everyday lived reality. I want to struggle with compartmentalization, with the desire to infuse my "public" life with my "private" ideas and beliefs—to bridge the secular and the sacred.

Lerner (2000) distinguishes, as do I, between spirituality and religion. He also is clear to distance his ideas from conservative religious politics with his distinction between "emancipatory" and "reactionary" spirituality (167–184). Lerner sees reactionary spirituality when one group asserts "the authoritative account of truth" (174). Reactionary spirituality also "rejects the claims of science and rational inquiry," and ends up supporting "the values of capital or those of the ruling elite," even as it pretends to "critique the values of capital" (175).

As a liberatory alternative to this retrograde trajectory, Lerner (2000) posits a view of spirituality that takes the form of resistance and struggle (179). It is a deep and abiding change in consciousness that will resist "the globalization of capital and the ethos of selfishness and materialism" (179). Unlike an ethereal or romanticized spirituality that promotes a "detached aesthetic," Lerner's view is grounded in the here and now. It cultivates "our capacities for awe and radical amazement" that "elicit a complete involvement of one's whole self" (167). This emancipatory spirituality is a lived experience, a set of practices and consciousness that involves, among other things,

- Cultivating our capacity to see each other as ends, not means to some other end;
- affirming the equal worth of every human being;
- healing and trans[forming] of the world, so that all of our public institutions cooperate to enhance peace ... ecological sanity, social justice ...;
- cultivating our capacity to transcend our individual egos;
- enhancing our capacity to play, to experience joy and pleasure, to honor our emotions and the emotions of others;
- encourag[ing] non-goal directed aesthetic creativity in music, dance, painting ... and other forms of human artistic expression;
- affirming pleasure and sexuality while rejecting all attempts to separate Spirit from its embeddedness in body;
- encouraging an overwhelming feeling of love toward others and a respectful caring for their needs, without forgetting our own needs;
- promot[ing] respect and care for the well-being of the entire universe, a desire to live ecologically sustainable lives;
- deepening of our intellectual capacities so they can be directed toward ensuring the survival and flourishing of the human race;
- integrat[ing] of our many capacities and strengths, both on the individual and global levels, without insisting that our unique traditions be subservient to some new universal view of "the single right way";
- changing the bottom line of society from an ethos of selfishness and materialism to an ethos of love and caring; (167–173).

Obviously, much of what Lerner addresses has come through the philosophical and religious work of generations of thinkers from all parts of the world. However, Lerner takes these general dimensions a step further and connects them to particular vocational or professional domains, including education. As a good teacher, a good rebbe, he advocates in his "spiritualization of education" many of the things we in educational studies profess (Lerner 2000, 195). In fact, I think there are many parallels between what Lerner would call a "spiritual teacher" and what we might call a "critical pedagogue." For example, Lerner implores us to move away from the market-driven analysis of education to a "new bottom line." In his admittedly utopian view, he challenges us to transform the dominant values of "competitive individualism, scientism, materialism, and selfishness" (235). Some of the particular positions he advocates include eliminating "the SAT and other odious forms of testing"; integrating "multiple forms of intelligence," including emotional intelligence, into our pedagogical situation; and educating for "awe and wonder at the sacred," for "love, caring and cooperation," as well as, of course, for tolerance, diversity, and citizenship (236–261).

Clearly these positions need elaboration. And certainly I don't pretend to be the first educational theorist to come to this loaded, even problematic, topic of spirituality. Much has been written, many paths already blazed, including by folks here at AESA. But it still remains a taboo place, a marginalized domain with too many of us. I want to take the risk with you, from this "bully pulpit," to continue this conversation, to open that hermeneutical space Gadamer speaks of, as we see from other horizons.

I want to invite connection over compartmentalization; to embrace the both/and; to insist on unity and diversity; to search for meaning in all we do; to resist the violence of objectification and categorization while maintaining some kind of critical consciousness; to attend to our entire be-ing in a way that doesn't privilege mind over body, thought over feeling; to allow generosity and love to surround our critical capacities. I want a dialogue that addresses the similarities and differences between the wisdom of a spiritual teacher and the radical analysis of a critical pedagogue.

The title of my talk refers to mind, body, and soul. We spend most of our time on/in "mind." More of us have begun to attend to the "body." And a few of us are devoting attention to the "soul." But this last category eludes clarity. Lerner helps again here. For him,

> Like Spirit, soul is one of those words that people never seem to want to define. And for good reason: *soul is not a thing,* not even an especially ghostly thing inside you. Rather, *it's a capacity*—but a capacity that cannot be explained in scientific terms [emphasis added]. In religious terms, the soul is what makes repentance and atonement possible. No past mistake will ever be bad enough to keep us from starting over and fundamentally transforming ourselves. The capacity for self-transformation and inner healing is part of what we mean by having a soul—the soul is the part of us that energizes us to go for our highest ethical and spiritual vision of who we can be. (2000, 9–10)

I am interested in talking about that capacity in our educational discourse—to take up the challenge presented by someone like Bob Kerrey; to reach for that element of forgiveness in the context of personal and social transformation. But unlike Kerrey, I think it must be about more than one's *personal* journey. We must overcome "the false dichotomy between changing ourselves and changing societal structures" (Lerner 2000, 273). For Lerner, and for me, "emancipatory spirituality encourages a *living synthesis* of individual and social transformation" (273). Informed by the praxis of *Tikkun Olam,* one must change *both* one's self *and* the world.

This connects, finally, to another Jewish teaching that helps me as an academic: that of the Sabbath, or making Shabbat. The traditional understanding is that for six days, we work to repair the earth, we engage in *Tikkun Olam;* on the seventh *we act as if the work is done*. This seventh day is a time for rest, for sex, for study, for fun with family and friends. Extending this we can reach for the *true meaning* of the *sabbatical year:* For six years we labor and in the seventh we stop—for "'let[ting your land] rest and lie fallow'" (Lerner 1994, 330). Historically this was supposed to be a time for individuals and communities to reflect; to rest; and to rejuvenate the mind, body, and soul. It was also a time to give the *earth* a rest—a period of ecological steward-ship where resources were renewed and balance was restored. This is a far cry from the contemporary academic sabbatical, where not only are we *not supposed* to rest, *but we are required to produce more work than ever!* For Lerner, "the sabbatical year becomes an important instruction to the human race: you don't run things, you are stewards, and you can have power to run your lives only if you do it in accord with the higher purpose that you are here to serve. Imagine the human race taking off one year out of every seven" (331). Now there's a radical thought!

Thank you for this opportunity to share these ideas. I welcome a dialogue. Shabbat Shalom. May you find peace. May you be at rest. May we be at peace. May we find rest. May the world find peace.

Acknowledgment

Some of the section "Bodily Knowing" appeared previously in "Critical Educa-tion and Embodied Subjects: Making the Poststructuralist Turn," *Educational The-ory,* 48 (4): 511–519, and "Educating for Emancipatory Rationality," in *Critical Conversations in Philosophy of Education* (1995, 103–115).

Notes

1. I am keeping this talk as I spoke it in Miami, even though months have passed and the ex-istential situation I now find myself in has changed since I wrote it. I no longer work at The New School or live in Hoboken, NJ.
2. This number has now been reduced officially to just less than 3,000.
3. I think here of Susan Bordo, Jane Gallop, Judith Butler, and Elizabeth Grosz, among oth-ers.
4. Lerner has been criticized, rightly I think, for a lack of attention to feminist and lesbian Jewish politics.
5. I realize my own contradictions even in making these linguistic distinctions/divisions.

References

Bordo, Susan. 1989. "The Body and the Reproduction of Femininity: A Feminist Appropri-ation of Foucault." Pp. 13–33 in *Gender/Body/Knowledge: Feminist Reconstructions of Being and Knowing.* Edited by Allison Jaggar and Susan Bordo. New Brunswick, N.J.: Rutgers University Press.

Britzman, Deborah. 1998. *Lost Subject, Contested Objects: Toward a Psychoanalytic Inquiry of Learning.* Albany: State University of New York Press.

DeMeo, James. 1998. *Saharasia: The 4,000 BCE Origins of Child Abuse, Sex-Repression, Warfare and Social Violence.* Ashland, Oreg.: Orgone Biophysical Research Lab.

Greene, Maxine. 1973. *Teacher as Stranger: Educational Philosophy for the Modern Age.* Belmont, Calif.: Wadsworth.

———. 1988. *The Dialectic of Freedom.* New York: Teachers College Press.

———. 1995. *Releasing the* Imagination: *Essays on Education, the Arts, and Social Change.* San Francisco: Jossey-Bass.

Grosz, Elizabeth. 1994. *Volatile Bodies: Toward a Corporeal Feminism.* Bloomington: Indiana University Press.

Harvey, Elizabeth, and Kathleen Okruhlik, eds. 1992. *Women and Reason.* Ann Arbor: University of Michigan Press.

Jones, Alison. 1996. "Desire, Sexual Harassment and Pedagogy in the University Classroom." *Theory Into Practice* 35 (2): 102–109.

Kohli, Wendy. 1984. *Toward Critical Hermeneutic Competence: The Empowerment of Teachers.* New York: Syracuse University.

———. 1995. *Critical Conversations in Philosophy of Education.* New York: Routledge.

———. 1998. "Critical Education and Embodied Subjects: Making the Poststructural Turn." *Educational Theory* 48 (4): 511–519.

Lerner, Michael. 1994. *Jewish Renewal: A Path to Healing and Transformation.* New York: Harper Perennial.

———. 2000. *Spirit Matters: Global Healing and the Wisdom of the Soul.* Charlottesville, Va.: Hampton Roads Publishing.

Lerner, Michael, and Cornell West. (1995). *Jews and Blacks: Let the Healing Begin.* New York: G.P. Putnam's Sons.

Lloyd, Genevieve. 1989. "The Man of Reason." Pp. 111–128 in *Women, Knowledge and Reality: Explorations in Feminist Philosophy.* Edited by Ann Garry and Marilyn Pearsall. Boston: Unwin Hyman, Inc.

Lorde, Audre. 1984. *Sister Outsider: Essays and Speeches by Audre Lorde.* Freedom, Calif.: The Crossing Press.

Said, Edward. 2001. "The Clash of Ignorance." *The Nation* (October 22): 12.

West, Cornell. 1993. *Race Matters.* Boston: Beacon Press.

Young, Iris Marion. 1990. *Throwing Like a Girl.* Bloomington: Indiana University Press.

Correspondence should be addressed to Wendy Kohli, 73 Mather Street, Hamden, CT 06517. E-mail: wendy.kohli@att.net

"Our World Will Never Be the Same." Let Us Hope So.

BILL GRIFFEN
Cortland State University of New York

Post 9/11 truisms reflect emerging positions on the effects of this catastrophic flash point event. Two of the more popular shibboleths collide to unmask a basic contradiction. "We must return to normalcy or the terrorists have won" struggles to coexist with "the world will never be the same" new abnormality view. Hidden, covert meanings in both clichés are probed and an argument is presented for rejecting a return to normalcy, a normalcy of U.S. hegemony continuing to manage, frequently violently, a global order that subverts the majority of the planet's human and environmental needs. Implications for schooling are discussed.

"United We Stand," shout a million American flag bumper stickers and window signs. Bill Moyers (2002) joins the chorus in celebrating how "Americans have rallied together in a way (not) remembered since World War II" (25). United and rallied together for what? As this is being written in early January 2002, Americans have fallen in step behind their newly appointed president and the military's bombing campaign, all aided by the noncritical, cheerleading media. There *was* a real need to unite in condemning the criminal (not war) attacks of 9/11 and in extending sympathy and support to all the families affected.

There is now a real need to try to understand why this happened. There is no shortage of explanations. The official government explanation continues in the imperium cold war vein that has driven most U.S. policy over the past two centuries: one more case of them against us, evil against good, barbarism against civilization, tyranny against freedom, enslavement against democracy. Once again, we have been attacked by aggressors and so the media saturates the under-attack TV audience with the hourly war cry: "America Strikes Back." President Bush and a compliant media bathe in the disbelief that anyone could visit this violence on a country as benevolent, caring, and dedicated to freedom throughout the world as America. Media commentators report, and, with very few exceptions, support, the entrenched view of "American exceptionality." Other nations act out of self-interest, while the U.S.A. is always liberating people, spreading democracy and advancing freedom across the globe. Some "others," incapable of our freedom-loving goodness, became so jealous of what we have and what we stand for that they committed unthinkable acts and killed innocent American civilians. Versions of this explanation made the media rounds and quickly became the main substance of the national conversation. The American Way of Life is under terrorist attack, and now more than ever, the battle lines are drawn between our good and their evil. Our president throws down the gauntlet: You're either with us or support terrorism and evil. Let the new war begin.

Let the spending for health needs recede even further; let the spending for warplanes and bombs increase. Let the spending on education continue on its snail-pace; let the spending for cash cow, unworkable "star war" schemes take off. Let the patriotic bowing to militarism increase; let the voices of nonviolence and negotiation be stilled. Let the "God Bless America" voices ring from every public gathering; let the "God Bless the World" voices be ignored and silenced. A few voices resist joining the patriotic chorus to remind us of the past historical reality, not the processed "history" shaped to the interests of the "let us return to normalcy by wrapping ourselves in the flag" present jingoism. These few voices, marginalized or ignored by mainstream media and therefore mostly silenced, remind us what is and has been normal for our culture, our foreign policy, and our role in the world, past and present.

Michael Lerner (2001) observes that "it's not that Americans are willfully deceiving themselves. Most Americans have never ever heard a serious presentation of our history and our current role in the world" (8). That history of U.S. terrorism has always been buried, marginalized, minimized, or distorted by those courting power, the big media (*The Nation* 2002). "Official History" replaces the real history. Policy decisions are legitimized by appeals to an idealized past that has been distorted and fictionalized to rationalize America's imperial agenda and to continue the "America is the exception" myth.

The real history is not censored in the traditional sense, it is censored by being ignored or dismissed as merely extremist, anti-American views. This lost and neglected history *is* available. It multiplied rapidly on the Internet in the weeks following 9/11, but the Official History–filtering system that moves information and interpretation on to the Larry King, *Hardball, Meet the Press,* MSNBC, Fox, CNN "one view fits all" info-tainment business, managed to ignore the Internet's diverse offerings. This points up the problem that even an open-to-all-views democratic cyberspace can be neutralized by the ubiquitous mass media. The alternative, independent press also delivered the real history record, only to be swallowed by the big official spin. Real history evidence dramatizes the unjust and immoral nature of establishing a national response to 9/11 based on historic lies and omissions.

> Since W.W. II, we have not hesitated to use the most powerful military in the world for political and/or economic gain in places like China (1945–46), Korea (1950–53), China (1950–53), Guatemala (1954), Indonesia (1958), Cuba (1959–60), Guatemala (1960) Congo (1964), Peru (1965), Laos (1964–73), Vietnam (1961–73), Cambodia (1969–70), Guatemala (1967–69), Grenada (1983), Libya (1986), El Salvador (1980s), Nicaragua (1980s), Panama (1989), Iraq (1991–present), Sudan (1998), Afghanistan (1998) and Yugoslavia (1999). We have bombed each of these countries in turn, and in NO case did a democratic government, respectful of human rights, occur as a direct result. Through our weapons and/or proxies, innocent civilians of Indonesia, East Timor, Chile, Nicaragua and Palestine have also been victims of the United States. Is it any wonder that the level of hatred of the United States is so high? (Thompson 2001)

This not-for-prime-time e-mail then reminds us of an earlier warning from President Carter of U.S. violent actions (some on his watch). One searches in vain, however, for the term "terrorism" to describe this violence.

More neglected history delivered on 9-22-01 from cyberspace answers the question "Why do 'they' hate us?" with overwhelming clarity, while the TV nets and cable struggle as if the question were on a level with "how did life begin?" Stephen R. Shalom (2002) presents a listing of specific incidents of U.S. use of force and threat of force in the Middle East. Whether these actions, military and economic, directly motivated "the horrific and utterly unjustified attacks of September 11 is unknown. But the grievances (that resulted) surely helped to create the environment which breeds anti-American terrorism." He then provides a *real* history from 1948 to 2000 that solves the mystery of "why?" created by the architects of official history.(2)

One of the most reliable documentors of recent history, Noam Chomsky (1988, 1992, 1994, 1999, 2001) reminds us that "in much of the world the U.S. is regarded as a leading terrorist state, and with good reason" (2001, 23). He recounts U.S. violent assaults against Nicaragua in the 1980s, U.S. support of Turkey's crushing of its own Kurdish population, the destruction in Sudan of the Al-Shifa pharmaceutical plant (it produced 90% of Sudan's pharmaceutical products) in 1998 (2001, 44–50), and, of course, the terror visited on Vietnam (for over four decades, Chomsky documented our terrorist role in Indochina). Edward Herman (2002) reminds us that why the populace doesn't see any of the above as terrorism is that "states define terrorism and identify the terrorists, and they naturally exempt themselves as always 'retaliating' and engaging in 'counter-terror' even when their own actions are an exact fit to their own definitions." (30)

"The scale and consequences of the September 11 attack are massive indeed, but this was not the worst act of mass terrorism in U.S. history—one must not forget that the atomic raids on Hiroshima and Nagasaki killed 210,000 people, most of them civilians, most perishing instantaneously" (Bello 2002, 51). Walden Bello, the writer of those words, argues that the purpose of the bombings had more to do with terrorizing and destroying the civilian population than destroying military targets.

A crucial part of making sense of real history, as opposed to bumper sticker, feel-good history, is the role economics plays in driving history. With all of the accomplishments of the capitalist economic engine, it must be noted that a human environmental price must be extracted. The accounting ledger represents a long history of social inequality. In the past few decades inequities have increased. Following is the picture in numbers. Sadly, this quantified misery list has the power to numb as well as enrage. Here is what "getting back to normal" means for the majority of earthlings:

- In 1900, people in the 10 richest nations earned nine times as much per capita as did people in the 10 poorest nations. By 1960, the ratio was 30 to 1. (In 2000, it was 72 to 1. Almost half the people on earth today live on less than $2 a day. (T)he three richest people on earth have wealth that exceeds the combined gross domestic product of the 43 poorest nations (*U.S. News & World Report,* 5/14/01, 68).

- Chief executive officer salaries in the United States rose by 571% between 1990 and 2000 while workers struggled with a 5% (adjusted for inflation) raise in the same period (Institute for Policy Studies, Washington, D.C.). Today's average CEO makes more than $12 million, 400 times that of a blue-collar worker (CBS.MarketWatch.com, 3/21/01).
- The wealth of the *Forbes 400* richest Americans grew $1.44 billion each from 1997 to 2000, for an average daily increase in wealth of $1,920,000 per person ($240,000 per hour or 46,602 times the U.S. minimum wage) (www.forbes.com).
- Funds in the hands of U.S. money managers grew from $1.9 trillion in 1980 to $17 trillion in 2000. The pay gap between top executives and production workers in the 362 largest U.S. companies soared from 42:1 in 1980 to 475:1 in 1999 (Gates 2002, 30).
- From 1983–1997, only the top 5% of U.S. households saw an increase in net worth, while wealth declined for everyone else (Gates 2002, 30).
- The financial wealth of the top 1% of U.S. households now exceeds the combined household financial wealth of the bottom 95% (Gates 2002, 30). The share of the nation's after-tax income received by the top 1% nearly doubled from 1979 to 1997. By 1998, the top-earning 1% had as much combined income as the 100 million Americans with the lowest earnings (Gates 2002, 31).
- Two billion people (1 out of 3) suffer from malnutrition, including 55 million in industrialized countries (Gates 2002, 31).

That was the normal world on September 10, 2001. This is the normal world today. Who in this normal world is the "us" as in the "us against them" world that President Bush calls for? Who is the "them"? Where do we place starving children and daily death victims of preventable disease on the terrorism ledger?

While the patriotic button-pushing from above reached frenzied levels and all attention was on September 11, the political owners of America paid off their corporate partners with a tax bill that gave IBM, General Motors, and General Electric a total of $3.27 billion in immediate tax rebates. The total gift to top corporate America was $25 billion, twice what the 37 million low-income families received. So the richest 1% got 41% of the new tax cuts and the bottom 60% got 7% (Citizens for Tax Justice).

The U.S. "us," in the "us against them" world, is about 4% of the population that continues to exhaust between 25 to 35% of the planet's resources. To sustain and protect that materially privileged position (grossly unequally shared, see above), "our economic system features long supply-lines, concentrated supplies of volatile fuels, toxic chemicals and radioactive materials, disposable workers subject to instant dismissal in a moment of disruption, core industries subject to extreme swings of consumer confidence, and an unstable financial system built on debt and speculation." David Korten, board chair of the Positive Futures Network, warns, "It is a disaster waiting to happen" (2002, 53). Actually, it's starting to happen.

In a deadly combination of naked self-interest, corporate America forges on with their globalization grand plan. What do the World Bank, the United Nations, and the Central Intelligence Agency have in common? They all agree that globalization increases worldwide poverty and inequality.

> Globalization appears to increase poverty and inequality. The costs of adjusting to greater openness are borne exclusively by the poor, regardless of how long the adjustment takes. (The World Bank, the Simultaneous Evolution of Growth and Inequality, 1999)

> The new rules of globalization—and the players writing them—focus on integrating global markets, neglecting the needs of people that markets cannot meet. The process is concentrating power and marginalizing the poor, both countries and people.... The current debate [about globalization] is ... too narrow, limited to the concerns of economic growth and financial stability and neglecting broader human concerns such as persistent global poverty, growing inequality between and within countries, exclusion of poor people and countries and persistent human rights abuses. (United Nations Human Development Report, 1999)

> The rising tide of the global economy will create many economic winners, but it will not lift all boats ... [It will] spawn conflicts at home and abroad, ensuring an even wider gap between regional winners and losers than exists today ... [Globalization's] evolution will be rocky, marked by chronic financial volatility and a widening economic divide.... Regions, countries, and groups feeling left behind will face deepening economic stagnation, political instability, and cultural alienation. They will foster political, ethnic, ideological, and religious extremism, along with the violence that often accompanies it. (United States Central Intelligence Agency)

Who does benefit from the current globalized economic system? "It's not the farmers driven from their lands and made into homeless refugees. It's not urban dwellers, dealing with influxes of displaced peoples, jamming in to look for jobs. It's not workers caught in downward wage spirals." And Jerry Mander (2001) adds, "It's surely not nature" (39). The benefactors of this system of exploiting nature and workers are the rich and super rich described in the first part of this essay. Mander challenges the popular fatalistic assumptions of inevitability by pointing out that "this process (globalization)—these institutions and the rules they operate by—have been created on purpose by human beings and corporations and economists and bankers, and have specific forms designed for specific outcomes. It is no accident. It was not inevitable. And it can be reversed or revised ..." (Mander 2001, 34).

To be educated today is to be able to expose the lies and half-truths of corporate-coded versions of reality, "official" reality. The question, "Who will benefit?" must be consistently raised. Ellen Reiss of the Aesthetic Realism Foundation lays bare this official deceit by correctly observing, "the principal purpose of U.S. international policy has been for the earth and its people to provide profit for U.S. corporations. That has meant 'supporting thugs and tyrants,' who are friendly to this purpose" (2001). In the official history, convenient collective amnesia serves our leaders well. When the thugs and tyrants serve our hegemonic agenda, they are used as allies. Political reincarnation is practiced as the 1980s anti-Communist freedom fighter, Osama bin Laden, is reborn now as the evil terrorist.

A careful reading of insider (aimed at elites) sources can help supplement and confirm the real history being preserved in the independent sources. *Foreign Affairs,* a journal aimed at the foreign policy establishment, offers a no-spin description of the reality surrounding the events of 9/11: "The American imperium in the Arab-Muslim world (beginning with the Gulf War) hatched a monster. ... Primacy (the term used for U.S. hegemony) begot its nemesis.... Arabia had been overrun by Americans, bin Laden said, 'For more than seven years the United States has been occupying the lands of Islam in the holiest of its territories, Arabia, plundering its riches, overwhelming its rulers, humiliating its people, threatening its neighbors, and using its peninsula as a spearhead to fight the neighboring Islamic peoples.'" The editors of the *Monthly Review* (2002) observe that "the more that the United States extends its empire in the Middle East/Islamic world, the more terrorist attacks will occur. Such realistic views, presented by the foreign policy establishment, are almost entirely absent in mass media accounts ..." (inside covers).

There are, I believe, several major messages connected to the events of 9/11. The most urgent is to sort out the basic contradiction between the establishment calls for "back to normal" and the contradictory mass cliché that "after September 11 nothing will be the same." For popular consumption, this is decoded to mean that our materialistic lifestyles, the American way of life, must not be threatened by these evil, freedom-hating terrorists. So, hit the malls and feed the market; in your face, evildoers! And the official mainstream "everything has changed" mantra means that there will now be a price to be paid for the U.S. top-of-the-heap world position. The "circle the wagons" takes us from the cold war to the good-versus-evil war. Security is the watchword and, for some, a new growth industry. We will spend our way to a safe and secure future as the military takes center stage, and the peace-through-force-and-violence industries crank up the military responses: more weapons, worthless missile umbrella shields, and the never-ending technology of new ways to efficiently kill. Unasked by officialdom: Are there no other paths than the cul-de-sac of cyclical war?

If the assumptions of official history prevail, the consequences will be an escalation of pauperism in the world, increasing the motivation and conditions for all forms of frustration-violence as victims are offered no other alternatives. Patriotic energies will be mobilized to continue in the cold war made of "us against them" jingoism. The official orchestrated reactions to 9/11 give us an emerging (long-term) terrorism cold war, increased militarism, heightened nationalism ("finally we're united"), and continuation of worship of the market, all leading to the elite's vaunted world order global capitalism. Over one-quarter of a century ago, Philip Slater (1974) was telling us that "our society is founded on pathological premises," and offered this metaphor: "Our culture is like a con man who persuades us to cheat those close to us of their due, and to invest instead in ourselves—we are still connected, but now through the con man" (187). The modern transformation to economic growth, profit-value (as opposed to use-value), and markets that dominate and shape our existence is responsible for driving the "con job" role of culture. Elsewhere I argued that the "fixation on the growth economy society as a way of organizing existence must be broken.... Karl Polanyi offered the thesis that the self-adjusting market 'could not exist for any length of time without annihilating the human and natural substance of society; it would have physically destroyed man and transformed his surroundings into a wilderness'" (Griffen 2000, 414).

If that "con job" culture that emerged from the agricultural revolution just 10,000 years ago were an automobile, it would be recalled. It has turned out to be more dangerous than a lemon. By human standards, by ecological standards, the debit side continues to accelerate. The achievements, and there are many (technological and nontechnological), can no longer justify the increasing threats and real disasters defining our new century. Whether it is billions of lives in sustained misery and poverty or the planet's life systems' degradation, one question is fundamental: Can we learn to imagine a world and an existence dramatically different from today's doomed civilization? We have help. Some *have* been taking those imaginative leaps and *concretely* offering outlines of what is needed. These are the people Morris Berman (2000) identifies as modern-day monastics.

Schools, because of their *relative* freedom to contemplate (critical thinking is encouraged, although seldom practiced) ought to support the "monastic" outlook on life. Berman cites Ernest Becker as a monastic disciple who has championed the nurturing of "the individual [who] reflexively sees through his or her own cultural conditioning and refuses to be blindly driven any longer by the heroic program of power and achievement. At this point, of liberation from the conditioning of culture, the individual comes face-to-face with the problem of the meaning of life, and can find no secure answer" (178).

Our materialistic-centered culture is a constant distraction from imagining other possibilities of living and being. Monastics, as a modern extension of their

Dark Age forbears, would sound the alarms. The small voices of urgency squeezing through the globalization cracks would serve as the canaries once did in the miners' shafts, warning about the hidden threats to life surrounding humans and their existence into the future.

Listen to some of the warning voices. Thom Hartmann (1999) characterizes today's modern culture as formed by what he calls "stories" (myths, beliefs, and paradigms). The stories continue to shape values that result in behavior, individual and collective, that is at the root of our culture's demise. He contrasts the two cultures. The present culture story:

> *We are not an integral part of the world, we are separate from it* [emphasis in original]. The Earth (and all of the plant and animal life on it) is something different from us. We call that different stuff "nature" and "wilderness," we call ourselves "mankind," "humankind," and "civilization." We are very clear in our vision of the difference between us and the rest of life on the planet—we are separate from it, superior to it, and a law unto ourselves. When we want something, it's there for us to take [my note: hence Daniel Quinn's, author of *Ishmael*, term of "takers" for post-agricultural revolution culture and "leavers" for hunter-gatherer civilizations], and we don't have to answer to anyone else. (119–120)

The pre-agricultural revolution culture story:

> We are part of the world [emphasis in original]. We are made of the same flesh as other animals. We eat the same plants. We share the same air, water, soil, and food with every other life form on the planet. We are born into life by the same means as other mammals, and when we die we, like them, become part of the soil which will nourish future generations. (154)

The accepting of one story over the other alters in the most basic way the existence and behavior of humans on this planet. The present culture story that we are trapped in, has moved us on these cultural paths:

> *It is our destiny to subdue and rule the rest of creation* [emphasis in original]. From the Bible's command to establish "dominion" over the Earth and its inhabitants, to the American government's acted-out doctrine of Manifest Destiny, to our science-fiction stories which express that we deserve to be the designated rulers of everything we can see, from the seas to the moon and beyond. Some people try to soften this by saying when Man was given dominion of the Earth, it meant he was given responsibility for taking care of it, but few people in our culture behave as if they believe this. (Hartmann 1999, 120)

The pre-agricultural revolution culture contains the following cultural lessons:

> *It is our destiny to cooperate with the rest of creation* [emphasis in original]. Every life-form has its purpose in the grand ecosystem, and all are to be respected. Each animal and plant has its own unique intelligence and spirit. We are permitted to *compete* with other plants and animals, but we may not wantonly *destroy* them. All life is absolutely sacred as is human life. Although hunting and killing for food are part of nature's order, when we do so it must be done with respect and thankfulness. (154–155) (see Quinn 1992, 127–132, for a discussion of the "law of limited competition")

Another monastic, against-the-grain voice of wisdom belongs to C. A. Bowers (1997, 2001). He has been using that voice for the past few decades to warn about the "guiding root metaphors that underlie the high-status knowledge" (accorded high-status knowledge for its use in socializing economic market addictions). Those root metaphors must be exposed, understood, and replaced by nonanthropocentric ones. Bowers sees the main root metaphors as

> 1. The pursuit of self-interest and the sense of being separate from nature ... 2. An anthropocentric view of the world.... 3. Change is viewed as inherently progressive in nature ... 4. Traditions ... are seen as inhibiting progress.... 5. The world is understood as secular in nature ... [limiting spirituality] ... 6. Social development is understood in economic and technological terms.... 7. Machines ... continue to serve as the analog for understanding life processes. (Bowers 1997, 6–7)

What Can Be Done?

Only the interests of the powerful few will be served by a return (continuation!) of normalcy. Use the belief that "nothing will be the same" as an opportunity to work for real change, outside the globalism-ecocide culture trap. The normalcy to be rejected is too scarred by poverty and its accompanying human misery to tolerate any longer, let alone support. The "justification" advanced for continuing a status quo normalcy that neglects the needs of the majority and their earth nest is the rationalization of the need for competitive greed (euphemistically altered) to motivate humans. And, of course, only the present "all against all" economic system, we are told, provides that motivation. Stretched to global dimensions, the competitive credo becomes the "us against them" world now being used to usher in the next round of wars. A world of such inequities and injustices will never see peace. Here is the soil for terrorism, nurtured by human-inflicted, culture-determined conditions. And here is where the "war on terrorism" must be waged. The incubators of terrorism, miserable living conditions, must be eliminated. Failure in our own domestic war on poverty should instruct us of the present system's failure. As part of the problem, corporate global-ism is a fatally flawed, doomed-to-failure nonsolution.

Moderns are trapped in an existence story (civilized culture) that sets us apart from the environment and each other. Modern cultural metaphors (anthropocentrism, progress materially defined, the autonomous individual) rein-force the distancing of ourselves from the natural as technology worship serves to further exacerbate modern alienation. Failure to understand commonalties among earthlings perpetuates divisive competitions expressed through cultural contexts of religions, nations, races, genders, and sexual and spiritual differences and orien-tations. A commonality is needed to render these culturally constructed differ-ences secondary.

A consciousness of self is considered normal and encouraged as individuals form their self-identities. The next stage could be the development of a consciousness of one's culture. Maslow's theory of individual development ("hierarchy of individual needs") moving through stages toward the apex of self-actualization would be dia-lectically joined with attention to a corresponding "hierarchy of cultural needs." Corresponding to the individual's highest goal of self-actualization would be eco-justice cultural goals supportive of cultural self-actualization. It would become apparent that a culture whose highest goal (stunted on the hierarchy scale) is the de-velopment of individuals encouraged to accumulate the most wealth and attendant fame (generally connected with exploiting nature), will always severely limit indi-vidual growth and development. Self-actualization coupled with culture actualiza-tion would positively affect both the individual and the social domain.

We have two basic choices: a continuation of our "reproduction theory" of edu-cation, wherein the student learns how to join the ongoing social order, or a "criti-cal theory" aimed at encouraging the study of the social order, thus becoming criti-cally conscious of one's culture so as to understand *why* she should join (support) the present culture and through conforming behavior, cooperate in reproducing it. The second choice offers the possibility that "why?" questions will unmask the shallow superficiality of the "how?" questions.

The choice *not* to join adds a voice to the monastic chorus. It might even be the hundredth monkey (look it up).

References

Bello, Walden. 2002. "In the Eyes of the World." *Yes! A Journal of Positive Futures*. (Win-ter).

Berman, Morris. 2000. *The Twilight of American Culture*. New York: Norton.

Bowers, C. A. 1997. *The Culture of Denial*. Albany: State University of New York Press.

———. 2001. *Educating for Eco-Justice and Community*. Athens and London: The Univer-sity of Georgia Press.

Chomsky, Noam. 1988. *The Culture of Terrorism*. Boston: South End.

———. 1992. *Deterring Democracy*. New York: Hill and Wang.

———. 1994. *World Orders, Old and New*. New York: Columbia University Press.

————. 1999. *Profits Over People*. New York: Seven Stories Press.

————. 2001. *9–11*. New York: Seven Stories Press.

Gates, Jeff. 2002. "Modern Fashion or Global Fascism?" *Tikkun* 17 (1).

Griffen, William. 2000. "Envisioning a Different Civilization: Education's Next Goal." *Educational Studies* 31:411–420.

Hartmann, Thom. 1999. *The Last Hours of Ancient Sunlight*. New York: Harmony Books.

Herman, Edward. 2002. "The Threat of Global State Terrorism." *Z Magazine* (January).

Institute for Policy Studies, Washington, D.C. (quoted in *The Washington Spectator*, Oct. 1, 2001, p. 4).

International Forum on Globalization (IFG). 2001. "Does Globalization Help the Poor?"

Keyes, Ken, Jr. 1981. *The Hundredth Monkey*. St. Mary, Ky.: Vision Books.

Korten, David. 2002. "Our Time to Choose." *Yes! A Journal of Positive Futures*. Winter (20): 53.

Lerner, Michael. 2001. "Healing After Terror." *Tikkun* 16 (6): 8.

Mander, Jerry. 2001. "Economic Globalization and the Environment." *Tikkun* 16 (5): 6.

Moyers, Bill. 2002. "Which America Will We Be Now?" *Utne Reader* (January–February): 25.

The Nation. 2002. "Big Media: And What You Can Do About It." Special issue, 274 (January 7/14).

Polanyi, Karl. 1944. *The Great Transformation*. Boston: Beacon.

Quinn, Daniel. 1992. *Ishmael*. New York: Bantam.

Reiss, Ellen. 2001. "Only Respect Will Win." "The Right of Aesthetic Realism To Be Known." Oct. 24, 2001, No. 1490.

Shalom, Stephen. 2001. "The United States and Middle East: Why Do They Hate Us?" E-mail.

Slater, Philip. 1974. *Earthwalk*. New York: Anchor.

Sweezy, Paul, et al., eds. 2002. "Notes from the Editors." *Monthly Review* 53 (8).

Thompson, Bill. 2001. "Combatting Terrorism." E-mail, September 12.

U.S. News & World Report (May 14): 68.

Zerzan, John, ed. 1999. *Against Civilization*. Eugene, Oreg.: Uncivilized Books.

Correspondence should be addressed to Bill Griffen, 7370 Palmer Road, Tully, NY 13159.

What Should We Tell Educators About Terrorism and Islam? Some Considerations in the Global Context After September 11, 2001

MARK GINSBURG and NAGWA MEGAHED
University of Pittsburgh

This article, stimulated by discussions at the 2001 American Educational Studies Association (AESA) conference, offers multiple perspectives on 2 separable topics, terrorism and Islam. It then suggests some challenges to teaching about these topics in Egypt, the Philippines, Cuba, and the United

States. Included in the challenges are the heterogeneity of people in each country and the complex historical and contemporary political/military dynamics within and between these countries.

This article is written by two internationally oriented sociologists of education,[1] who have been active in the Pittsburgh, Pennsylvania, "Mobilization for Peace" (since its founding meeting on September 23, 2001). We were involved together in a variety of meetings and events, and we also took responsibility separately for two educational efforts. Mark was invited by the instructors to speak to the Department of Administrative and Policy Studies Doctoral "Core" course on September 18, to discuss the preplanned topic of multiple perspectives and to open up a conversation about the issues arising out of the events of September 11. Nagwa was recruited by the World Affairs Council of Pittsburgh to address two classes at a high school in the Pittsburgh city school district on November 30, on the topic of "Understanding Islam and Arab Culture." These various experiences—and our participant observations during and between sessions (e.g., Greene 2002; Kohli 2002) at the AESA conference in Miami, Florida, October 31 to November 4, 2001—led us to the question in the title of this essay.

For purposes of discussion here, we want to consider the issues related to two separable topics (terrorism and Islam) that we believe need to be addressed as part of the content in preservice and inservice social foundations of education courses. Certainly, educators and their occupational socialization have a strong, if not always acknowledged, political dimension (Ginsburg 1995; Ginsburg and Lindsay 1995), and thus such topics constitute a relevant focus. This is not only because of the enormity of the death and destruction that occurred within U.S. territory as a consequence of the hijacking and crashing of four commercial airliners or because of the way many people have defined these events as a turning point in contemporary world history (e.g., see Lewis 2001; Marvel and McKenzie 2001). These topics (and others such as capitalism, Christianity, Judaism, revolution, and socialism) are salient in any attempt to understand the global social context of education (Burbules and Torres 2000; Gutek 1997; Stromquist and Monkman 2000).

Multiple Perspectives on Terrorism and Islam

To stimulate social foundations colleagues to consider what to discuss with educators, we present below some of the issues associated with the topics of terrorism and Islam. Because we are committed to critical pedagogy (Giroux 1997; Kanpol 1999; Luke and Gore 1992), we offer multiple perspectives on the issues.

Terrorism

In dictionaries the word *terrorism* has been defined as "threats or acts of violence, esp[ecially] as a means of intimidating or coercing" (*Funk and Wagnalls* 1980, 835) that can serve as "a mode of [either] governing or opposing government" (*Webster's* 1961, 877). However, at least in the United States "[d]uring the Reagan years [1980–1988], the simple term 'terrorism' ... became short-hand for any perceived threat of violence directed at U.S. interests" (Kawell 2001, 51; see also Herman 1982). This bipolar, but unidirectional conception of "terrorism" was clearly enunciated by U.S. President George W. Bush in his September 20, 2001,[2] television address to a joint session of Congress when he asserted that "there are thousands of these terrorists in more than sixty countries" and then stated: "Every nation in every region now has a decision to make. Either you are with us, or you are with the terrorists. From this day forward, any nation that continues to harbor or support terrorism will be regarded by the United States as a hostile regime" (quoted in "After the Attack" 2001, 4).[3]

We agree that the actions allegedly perpetrated by members of Osama bin Laden's al-Qaeda network on September 11, 2001, should be considered acts of terrorism against the U.S. government, as were the bombings of the U.S. Marines barracks in Beirut, Lebanon, on October 23, 1983; the World Trade Center in New York City (USA) on February 26, 1993; and the U.S. embassies in Nairobi, Kenya, and Dar es Salaam, Tanzania, on August 7, 1998 (see Kahn 2001). But we cannot agree that terrorism is directed only at the United States and its allies and we join in criticizing "[s]uccessive U.S. administrations ... for using an overly narrow definition of terrorism—the killing of noncombatants by individuals or small groups of irregulars—while ignoring the usually more widespread killings of equally innocent people by sanctioned organs of recognized states" (Zunes 2001, 1).

Many leaders and other citizens in the United States may disagree, but Amnesty International (1998) has reported "that the United States was as responsible for extreme violations of human rights around the globe—including the promotion of torture and terrorism and the use of state violence—as any government or organization in the world" ("After the Attack" 2001, 9). In a recently published article, McSherry summarizes the historical evidence of terrorism committed by the U.S. government and its allies:

> As McClintock [1991, 121, 130] noted, U.S. counterinsurgency doctrine and operations [initially developed and deployed after World War II in Europe] essentially legitimized the use of state terror.... Moreover, as Jeffrey A. Sluka [2000, 9] has pointed out, "the structures, tactics, and technology of state terror have been diffused, in fact aggressively marketed and exported as a form of 'military aid' to developing countries." (2002, 42, 56)

Thus, the appellation of a violent act as an act of "terrorism" involves a subjective interpretation (Juergensmeyer 2000). Ironically, "terrorism" like "beauty" is in the eye of the beholder. It is more likely that the acts of "others"—rather than one's own or one's allies' acts—are considered to constitute "terrorism" (Herman 1982).

Discussions of terrorism are complicated, moreover, because of differences in how violence is conceived (see Ginsburg et al. 1998), especially since the "most basic pattern is for defenders of constituted authority to use more restrictive definitions of violence and for opponents of constituted authority to use broader definitions" (Grundy and Weinstein 1974, 113). Generally, the concept of violence is associated with "acts of physical force aimed at severe injury or destruction of persons, objects or organizations" (Spiegel 1971, 20). In contrast or in addition to physical forms of violence, there is what some term "structural" violence (Galtung 1969), that is, "nonphysical acts of 'violation'" (Sanford 1971, 44) or violation of "the most fundamental natural rights of persons" (Garver 1968, 819). At a macrolevel, structural violence could involve governmental or other institutional policies and practices that create or perpetuate hunger, illness, illiteracy, or environmental degradation or otherwise cause premature death and/or diminish the quality of people's life (see Brock-Utne 1989). Thus, government agencies, international financial organizations, transnational corporations, and so on, can be seen to engage in structural violence—even "terrorism," if such violence is used "as a means of intimidating or coercing"—when they pursue policies that deprive people of food, medical care, education, or a sustainable environment.

Especially given a conception of terrorism that is not limited to the actions of our enemies and that includes structural as well as physical violence, we agree with Zunes (2001) that "[t]here is nothing inherent in Islamic, Middle Eastern, ... or any other tradition that spawns terrorism"[4] (1). And we would add that there is nothing inherent in any religious or cultural tradition that prevents it from being used to motivate violence or terrorism. For example, although the doctrines of all major religions promote peaceful relations, groups associated with various religions have claimed that their acts of violence and "terrorism" are justified by their religious faith (Hunter 1998; Juergensmeyer 2000).[5] Therefore, although it may be dispiriting, it should not surprise us that Osama bin Laden issued an edict calling "on every Muslim ... to comply with God's order to kill the Americans and plunder their money wherever and whenever they find it" (Frontline 2001) and that George W. Bush exclaimed on September 20, 2001, that the United States would use "every necessary weapon of war" against the enemies, adding that "'God is not neutral'" (quoted in "After the Attack" 2001, 4).

Islam

"The word *Islam* derives from the three-consonant Arabic root *SLM*," (Arab World and Islamic Resources [AWIR] and Middle East Policy Council [MEPC] 1998, 1) "which generates words with interrelated meanings, including 'surrender,' 'submission,' 'commitment' and 'peace'" (Council on Islamic Education [CIE] 1995, 1). Thus, "Islam means the state of submission to the one and only God 'Allah,' and Muslim[6] refers to a person who has submitted to the will of Allah" (Chand 1992, 3). For believers, Islam is not a new religion but is rather the last reiteration of the primordial message of God's Oneness that God revealed through prophets associated with Judaic and Christian traditions[7] as well as through the Prophet Muhammad (CIE 1995; Voll 1994). Soon after Muhammad's death the records of God's revelations (via angel Gabriel) to Muhammad were collected and put in a standardized form, the *Qur'an* (AWIR and MEPC 1998; Council on American-Islamic Relations [CAIR] 2001; CIE 1995; Islamic Institute 2001; Voll 1994).

For Muslims, Islam is both a religion and a method of life. In addition to the *Qur'an,* there are three other sources of Islamic law *(Shari'a)*: (a) the *hadith,* which contains the *Sunnah* or life examples of the Prophet Muhammad; (b) the *Ijma* or consensus of the community of Islamic scholars in a given society and era; and (c) *Qiyas* (analogy), applying an injunction that applies in one case to another similar case (Islam Today 2001). Because of variations in scholars' interpretations and in individuals' choices of action, there are similarities as well as differences in the practice of some Islamic rules across societies and within a given society (AWIR and MEPC 1998; Glaberson 2001; Islam Today 2001). Moreover, under the belief in the Judgment Day and individual accountability for actions, Muslims are considered responsible for their own activities and thus exercise a degree of freedom. To illustrate the relationship between Islamic law, group differences in interpretation, freedom, and personal choice, we discuss below two Islamic rules that are viewed by some as contradicting Judeo-Christian or "Western" ideas of liberty and modernization: *hijab* (veiling of women) and *Jihad* (directed struggle). These discussions provide illustrations of multiple perspectives on and within Islam.

The word *hijab* comes from the Arabic word *hajaba,* meaning "to hide from view or conceal." The *Qur'an* and the *hadith* do not present a fixed standard for the type of clothing that Muslims must wear. However, they specify that some requirements of modesty must be met: (a) women's clothing should be loose and thick enough so as not to reveal the shape of their bodies *and* (b) men's clothing should not be too tight or provocative (Ali, Mary 2001). Modesty in clothing is important not only as an expression of commitment to God, but also because both men and women should be evaluated for their intelligence and skills instead of their looks and sexuality (Ali, Mary 2001; Doi 2001; Joan 1999). Some people (both Muslims and non-Muslims) view *hijab* as liberating for women, while other people (both Muslims and non-Muslims) view this Islamic rule as being oppressive, especially of women. Cook represents the former view in commenting that "[t]he *hijab* is important in Islamic society ... as a symbol of a women's commitment to God and as a form of protection from the unwanted advances of men" (2001, 401). In contrast, the latter view is signaled by the statement that "the most visible symbol of the Taliban's oppressive regime [in Afghanistan] was the order that placed all women under the *burka*"—"the head-to-toe garment ... a kind of body bag for the living" (Lacayo 2001, 38, 36).[8] It is important to point out that there are variations among Muslim societies and among individual Muslims in what, if any, head covering (e.g., a scarf, a veil, a *burka*) is required to maintain a woman's modesty. And in

Afghanistan under the Taliban (Lacayo 2001) as well as in other societies (Pinn 2000; Zuhur 1995;), Muslim women differ regarding whether they are covering their heads (and other parts of their bodies) because of personal choice; duty to God; or coercion/oppression by family members, religious leaders, and/or government officials.[9]

The Arabic word *jihad* is derived from the three consonants *JHD,* and its literal meaning is "exertion of effort or directed struggle" (AWIR and MEPC 1998, 3). "It is a central and broad Islamic concept that includes struggle against evil inclinations within oneself, struggle to improve the quality of life in society, struggle in the battlefield for self-defense" (CAIR 2001). Some people (both Muslims and non-Muslims) define *jihad* as "holy war," directed either against people and governments seen to be "un-Islamic"[10] or against the forces of "modernization" (Barber 2001). However, according to Islamic teachings, it is unholy to instigate or start war, although some wars are inevitable and justifiable (Ali, Amir 2001). Islamic law forbids and condemns wars of extermination or territorial conquest, but the *Qur'an* states that it is a religious duty for the entire Muslim community, women as well as men, to struggle (against people who attack first) in self-defense to protect life, property, and freedom. As with the case of *hijab,* one can see that, in the case of *jihad,* interpretations and choices have to be made. For example, when is an act of violence justified as self-defense and when is it an offensive action, an initial act of violence, a form of revenge, or an action in anger? Although individuals and groups can reach their own conclusions, it may be difficult to reach consensus on such issues. This only reminds us that there is not a single, monolithic version of Islam, and it is not appropriate to condemn or applaud Islam based only on the actions of one group that identifies itself as Muslim (Arkoun and Steinbach 2000).

Audiences in Different Contexts

In reading the discussion about what educators might be told about the separable topics of terrorism and Islam, presumably you considered the issues identified with at least some vague conception of the audience and context. That is, you likely supplied answers to questions such as the following: In what region of what country am I teaching social foundations of education? Who are the preservice or inservice educators with whom I am interacting? Who are the students these educators will encounter in their classrooms? Although we are not suggesting that what one tells educators about these issues should vary significantly in relation to differences in audience or context, we do believe that it is important to consider audience and context in anticipating how educators and their prospective students will interpret and respond to the issues raised. Here we focus on Egypt, the Philippines, Cuba, and the United States, exploring variations in audiences across and within societal contexts.

Egypt

Egypt is considered a Middle Eastern country located in the northeast corner of Africa. It has a population of over 69 million people, most of whom are Arabs with small minorities of Bedouins and Nubians. There are also important rural/urban, age, and social class differences among Egyptians. Islam is the official religion of Egypt, and Muslims (mostly of the Sunni tradition) constitute 90% of the population, though other religious groups, including the next largest group, Coptic Christians, are legally granted freedom of worship. The heterogeneity among Egyptians must be considered in teaching Egyptian educators about terrorism and Islam; however, perhaps more significant is the long-term, often violent conflict involving some groups of Muslims.

Of these groups, which developed initially during the British colonialism (1882–1922) and then after Egypt's independence continued to confront the monarchies of Ahmed Fuad Pasha (1922–1936) and Farouk (1936–1952) as well as the postrevolutionary governments of Gamal Adb El-Nasser (1952–1970), Anwar al-Sadat (1970–1981), and Hosni Mubarak (1981–present), the most well-known is *al-Ikhwan al-Muslimun,* or the Muslim Brotherhood, which was founded in 1928 by a schoolteacher, Hasan al-Banna (Voll 1994). Before the 1952 revolution, the Muslim Brotherhood grew rapidly and developed into a militant mass movement, viewed to have been the most powerful among radical university student and worker groups (of Muslims and non-Muslims), including those led by Marxists (Ibrahim 1987; Voll 1994).[11] After the 1952 revolution, "the Muslim Brotherhood issued a declaration of support for the revolution's leaders [and] ... repeatedly proclaimed the need for basing the new government on Islam" (Ibrahim 1987, 122). In 1954, when the Brotherhood and other radical groups challenged his government's decision to alter the Suez Canal Treaty with Britain, Nasser ordered that thousands of their members be imprisoned (without trial). Nasser also initiated a policy of secularization, for example, bringing religious courts and Al-Azhar University under secular state control (Ibrahim 1987)—actions that reinforced the Brotherhood's perception that the government of Egypt was "un-Islamic." This perception was further strengthened because of the increasing military and economic influence of the Soviet Union, especially after the 1956 war over control of the Suez Canal and the 1967 war between Israel and Egypt (as well as Jordan and Syria).

Perhaps ironically, in the 1970s when Sadat's government sought to address Egypt's pressing economic problems by encouraging Western European and North American investment, Sadat also empowered once again the Muslim Brotherhood, particularly among university students, as a political force opposing the Nasserists and other leftist groups—a strategy that had the support of both Saudi Arabia and the United States (Ibrahim 1987; Rubin 1997). At the same time, to make Egypt more attractive to such investment, Sadat dramatically scaled back relations with the Soviet Union and pursued peace with Israel (before and after the 1973 war). The *Al-Jama'at al-Islamiyya,* the Islamic groups that Sadat helped to create out of the Muslim Brotherhood, supported Sadat's moves to weaken the role of ("atheist/Marxist") Nasserists in Egypt and to distance Egypt from the Soviet Union, which not only was an atheist empire but also invaded the Muslim-majority nation of Afghanistan in 1979.[12] However, *al-Jama'at al-Islamiyya* opposed Sadat's efforts to establish peace with Israel, a major factor instigating his being assassinated in 1981 (Chomsky 2001; Dunn 1995; Federal Research Division 1990, chap. 2, pt. 4; Ibrahim 1987; Rubin 1997; Tschirgi 1999). This initial "terrorist" act was followed by a wave of "terrorism" in the 1980s and 1990s, directed especially at Egyptian government officials. For example, one or the other of the subgroups associated with *al-Jama'at al-Islamiyya*[13] is said to be responsible for killing the Minister of the Interior in 1984 and the Speaker of the Assembly in 1990; for injuring the Minister of Information in 1993; and for undertaking the attempted assassination of President Mubarak in Ethiopia on June 26, 1995 (Dunn 1995; FORSNET 2000; Juergensmeyer 1995).

Mubarak, the president of Egypt since 1981, during a period of increased military and economic aid from the United States,[14] "rejected any possibility of negotiation [with *al-Jama'at al-Islamiyya*]. Instead [his government] relied on heavy security measures, including massive arrests, the death penalty, ... the use of military courts to try suspected militants ... [and armed attacks], particularly in Upper Egypt" (Tschirgi 1999, 221, 228).[15] And in 1996 the Egyptian government rejected a call for cease-fire from some leaders of *al-Jama'at al-Islamiyya* groups and continued its intensive security approach. In November 1997, members of *al-Jama'at al-Islamiyya* groups slaughtered fifty-eight foreign tourists and some Egyptians in the city of Luxor—an attack that had a major negative impact on tourism, a major component of the Egyptian economy. Because President Mubarak was convinced that an international network was behind these terrorist attacks in Egypt, he called in 1997 for international action against terrorism—a call that was not fully heeded until the events of September 11, 2001.

This long, complex history of conflict and violence obviously presents challenges in teaching Egyptian educators about terrorism and Islam. It is not just that "'Egyptians are victims of terrorism as well,'" as stated by an aide of Muhammad Sayed Tantawi, "the highest ranking cleric in Egypt and an influential figure across the Sunni Islamic world," in explaining the level of security for his boss, "known as Shiekh of Al-Azhar" (Goldberg 2001, 53). It is that although some view *al-Jama'at al-Islamiyya* as a terrorist group falsely basing its actions on Islam, others perceive the Egyptian government (and its allies, Israel and the United States) as an un-Islamic terrorist state. Moreover, although Egypt has for years been labeled as "a major enemy of the bin Laden network" (Chomsky 2001, 11) and "less than a month before [September 11, 2001] ... Al-Qaida chieftains received a report spelling out 'exceptionally good opportunities' for terrorism in ... Egypt" (Cullison and Higgins 2002), "Egyptians are among those allegedly involved in the [September 11] attacks" (Goldberg 2001, 48).[16]

Philippines

The Philippines is a country located in the Asia-Pacific region, comprised of over 7,000 islands (ten of which contain 95% of the population) and inhabited by approximately 76.5 million people who speak "70 languages ... of which eight to ten are major ones" (Danskin 1979, 315). Although approximately 90% of the population and the dominant economic and political groups in the Philippines are Christian, Muslims have for centuries had an important presence, especially in the southern islands of the Philippines.[17]

The Philippines is a country that has a complex connection to topics of terrorism and Islam. Indeed, in December 2001, it was reported that one of the "new fronts in the war on terrorism" could be the Philippine island of Mindanao, which has a "large Muslim population with extremist elements ... linked to the global web of Islamic terrorism" (Dorgan 2001, A-27). And on January 8, 2002, we learned that "[t]he war on terrorism after Afghanistan could focus on ... the Philippine [island of Basilan], where ... the government [is] eager to quell a rebellion by hundreds of Muslim militants from the Abu Sayyaf group who have been linked to Al-Qaida and have been battling government forces" (Dao and Schmitt 2002, A1, A18). And just as we were finalizing this article, we read on January 16, 2002, that "U.S. Special Forces have begun arriving in the Philippines to assist Philippine troops in their fight against Muslim guerrillas linked to Osama bin Laden" (Vogel 2002, A8), "the first major expansion of the war on terrorism" (Schmitt 2002, A1).

Thus, in planning social foundations of education lessons on the topics discussed above, one would need to consider the Christian versus Muslim division among Filipinos as well as other dimensions of difference and stratification: rural/urban, social class, and so forth. But teaching in the Philippines about terrorism and Islam, especially in relation to the United States, is even more complicated because of the longer history of relations between these two countries. Here we draw on the very interesting analysis by Jeffrey Ayala Milligan, which he presented at the 2001 AESA conference, to sketch the nature of these relations. Milligan notes that, similar to the case of Cuba (see following),

> The United States arrived in the Philippines in 1898 as a result of its general assault on Spanish possessions in the Spanish-American War. At the moment ... Filipino insurgents had been engaged in a two-year struggle to claim their independence from Spain [after nearly 400 years as a Spanish colony] and had succeeded in bottling up most Spanish forces in urban garrisons. ... Two months after the Philippines was ceded to the U.S. in the Treaty of Paris in December of 1898, fighting erupted between U.S. troops and forces of the newly declared Philippine Republic ... raging for at least four more years and claiming the lives of up to 600,000 Filipinos and more than 5,000 Americans. (2001, 3)

Although the resistance to U.S. presence in the Philippines by Christian "freedom fighters" or "terrorists" in the north ended within a few years as the United States granted increasing degrees of political (if not economic) independence to a Christian-dominated Philippine government (fully granted on July 4, 1946), the struggle by Muslims against the United States and its Philippine government allies has continued until today.[18]

What is interesting about U.S. relations with the Muslim population in the Philippines—and relevant to our considerations here of what to tell teachers about terrorism and Islam—are the parallels between the discourse of the U.S. officials responsible for administering the territory and organizing education[19] to quell the resistance in the southern Philippines in the early decades of the twentieth century and the discourse of U.S. officials responsible for orchestrating the "war on terrorism" in Afghanistan at the beginning of the twenty-first century. According to Milligan,

> The great bulk of the writing on Muslim Filipinos in the period between 1898 and 1925 reinforced this conception of culture as a continuum between barbarism and civilization with "Moros"[20] and Americans at opposite ends [and Christian Filipinos somewhere in between].... Other authors emphasized the dangers of Muslim Filipino violence, highlighting their fighting prowess and the *juramentado,* a ritualized, suicidal attack on non-Muslim invaders.... Such accounts served ... [to] position the American soldier or civilian in Mindanao as a courageous defender of civilization. (2001, 7–8)

Moreover, much like the characterization of the Taliban and Al-Qaida groups targeted in today's "war on terrorism," it was claimed by U.S. officials during the early twentieth century that "Muslim Filipinos' Islamic identity ... [was only] a 'veneer' ... [because] they are not 'real Muslims' and know very little about their faith" (Milligan 2001, 10).

Cuba

Cuba is an Caribbean island nation of approximately 11 million people, who are heterogeneous with respect to race (Serrano Peralta 1995),[21] religious beliefs and practices (e.g., see Golden 1998; Miller 1996),[22] age/generation (Domínguez García 1997), Communist Party (non)membership, and rural/urban residence. Wealth/income differences exist but the reduction of such differences within and between rural and urban settings is acknowledged as "[t]he third great area of change [in addition to education and health care] presided over by the Revolution" (Semester at Sea 1999, 15). These characteristics of the population need to be considered when teaching Cuban educators about terrorism and Islam.

Moreover, teaching about these topics, especially as they are connected with the United States, is complicated because of the long and often conflict-laden history of relations between Cuba and the United States. As might be expected by its location, ninety miles south of the coast of Florida, this history predates the 1895–1898 Cuban independence struggle, which ended Spain's four-hundred-year colonization of the island. However, as with the case of the Philippines (see previous section), at this point (in the context of the Spanish-American War) the United States undertook a military occupation to "free" Cuba (Perez 1998), signed a treaty allowing in perpetuity a U.S. military base on the island at Guantánamo, and then in alliance with a series of "friendly" regimes became a dominant economic force in Cuba (Rius 1970). Cuba's 1959 revolution, which brought to power the July 26 Movement led by Fidel Castro, altered the relationship between Cuba and the United States (Rius 1970). Perhaps most important in this regard is the U.S. embargo on trade with and travel to Cuba, initiated in the early 1960s and more recently strengthened in 1992 by the Torricelli law ("The Cuba Democracy Act") and in 1996 by the Helms-Burton law ("The Cuban Liberty and Democratic Solidarity Act").

Teaching Cuban educators about terrorism and Islam is complicated, therefore, because, since January 11, 2002, the U.S. Naval Base at Guantánamo, Cuba, has been used as a prison for the "worst elements of the Al-Qaida and the Taliban" who were captured during "the U.S.-led war in Afghanistan" (Pressley 2002, A4, A1). Teaching about these topics in Cuba presents challenges also because

> Cuba continues to be one of seven governments designated by the [U.S.] State Department as "state sponsors of international terrorism"—the others being Iran, Iraq, Syria, Libya, North Korea and Sudan.... [And the September 11] attacks in the United States ... could provide Washington with a handy pretext for intensifying campaigns against ... Cuba.... (Kawell 2001, 50–51)[23]

Thus, despite Cuba's statement on September 11 expressing its "grief and sadness [over] the violent, surprise attacks carried out ... against civilian and official facilities in the cities of New York and Washington which has caused numerous deaths" as well as "strongly reject[ing] and condemn[ing] the attacks" (Government of Cuba [GOC] 2001b, 1), "Cuba is on the list [of terrorist countries] while Afghanistan is not" (Kalwell 2001, 53).

The September 11 statement by the Cuban government, however, also reminds us "that for over 40 years [Cuba] has been a victim of [terrorist] actions fostered from within the territory of the United States" (GOC 2001b, 1). There are hundreds of documented acts of physical violence[24] directed at Cuba, including bombings of buildings, destruction of crops, and attempts to assassinate its president, Fidel Castro (see Herman 1982; Kawell 2001; Robinson 1998). These acts by "terrorists" or "freedom fighters" began soon after the 1959 revolution, when "right-wing Cuban exiles were organized by the Central Intelligence Agency (CIA) to conduct a series of attacks inside Cuba that resulted in widespread civilian casualties" (Zunes 2001, 1). Perhaps the most (in)famous action was the April 1961 Bay of Pigs (*Playa*

Girón) invasion. Ironically, but probably not accidentally, this failed effort to reverse the Cuban revolution occurred in what Cubans officially called the "Year of Education" (Barnes 2001, 9). As Rius reports,

> On April 10, 1961, 20 thousand literacy workers of all ages spread out over the island to teach reading and writing to one million illiterates and by December ... Cuba had lowered the illiteracy rate from 24% to 3%.... On April 15 ... fleets of American warplanes painted with insignias of the Cuban Air Force bombed ... airports, trying to wipe out the [Cuban] Revolutionary Air Force.... And in the early morning of the 17th, 1500 mercenaries invaded the island, with 5 American ships, 2 battleships and 3 freighters loaded with tanks and artillery, coming from Nicaragua and escorted by 2 destroyers of the U.S. Navy. (1970, 116–117)

"Counterrevolutionary" acts of lesser magnitude have continued to this day, championed by a group of Cuban Americans (Landau and Smith 2001). Thus, the fact that many Cubans have relatives in the United States, some of whom wield considerable political and economic power in their "anti-Castro" pursuits (Hernández Martínez 1997),[25] further complicates decisions about how to approach teaching Cuban educators about terrorism. Personal feelings of love and hatred for one's relatives living in the United States would obviously intervene in teachers' and their students' interpretation of what are and what are not legitimate acts of violence.

United States

The United States of America, a North American society, has a population of more than 250 million people, composed of non-Hispanic Whites (approximately 71%), Hispanics (12%), non-Hispanic Blacks (11%), Asian (4%), American Indian and others (2%) (U.S. Census 1990, as reported in *World Book 2001 CD*). The population is also varied with respect to rural/urban residence, region, age, and social class. It is important to note that both race/ethnicity and social class are highly related to inequalities in wealth/income and political power (Braun 1997; Domhoff 1998; Marger 1997) as well as to differential participation in "volunteer" military service. In terms of religion, as of 1990, 60% of the population identified themselves as members of organized religious groups; and of these their affiliations were: various Protestant denominations (52%), Roman Catholic (37%), Jewish (4%), Mormon (3%), and Eastern Orthodox (3%), as well as less than 1% Muslims, Buddhists, and others (U.S. Census 1990, as reported in *World Book 2001 CD*). Since 1990, however, the Muslim population has grown rapidly—through conversion[26] and new migration from various regions of the world, such that by the end of the twentieth century, it was estimated that there were between 6 and 7 million Muslims in America, "making them the second largest religious group in the United States, after Christians" (AWIR and MEPC 1998, 4; see also CAIR 2001).[27]

These characteristics are critical to consider in terms of anticipating how educators and their students in the United States might respond to efforts to teach about terrorism and Islam. For example, contemplate the task of teaching U.S. educators about these topics when they and the students in the schools in which they work are white, black, and brown Muslim and non-Muslim U.S. citizens from families representing different social classes and political ideologies. And what about classrooms with some students who are non–U.S. citizens, such as a young boy living in Pittsburgh, while his mother pursues her doctorate, who is dropped off at school by his parents, who (since September 11) have attached an American flag to their car in order to avoid being attacked or hassled?

Teaching about these topics in the United States, however, is even more challenging because of the complexity of U.S. society and the contradictory nature of the foreign and domestic policies of the U.S. government. The society and these policies might be characterized as "America's contradictions, its on-again, off-again interest in extending rights, its clumsy egalitarianism coupled with ignorant arrogance," with the United States being viewed as a "freedom-loving, brutal, tolerant, shortsighted, selfish, generous, trigger-happy, dumb, glorious, fat-headed, powerhouse" (Gitlin 2002, 25, 24). This point is highlighted by Amnesty International:

> The USA was founded in the name of democracy, political and legal equality, and individual freedom. However, despite its claims to international leadership in the field of human rights, and its many institutions to protect individual civil liberties, the USA is failing to deliver the fundamental promise of rights for all. (1998, chap. 1)

Engaging U.S. educators in a discussion about terrorism is complicated because, although the United States is currently leading a "war against terrorism" and although (according to opinion polls) a large majority of the U.S. population has supported at least the initial military action in Afghanistan, some people (as noted above) might view the U.S. government, historically and today, as a perpetrator of state terrorism. "The United States has employed its military forces in other countries over seventy times since 1945, not counting innumerable instances of counterinsurgency operations by the CIA" ("After the Attack" 2001, 1–2). But the questions likely to be debated within Social Foundations of Education and other classrooms are what the purposes of these military actions were and in whose interests they were undertaken. Similarly, the U.S. government sends billions of dollars in aid, particularly to "developing" countries, but there are differences of opinion regarding whether such efforts are to improve the quality of life of impoverished people and/or to protect the investments of U.S.-based multinational corporations and strengthen U.S. hegemony.[28]

Teaching U.S. educators about terrorism and Islam is also difficult given what has happened in the U.S. since September 11. Certainly, we have witnessed an outpouring of charitable and humanitarian actions for those who were killed or lost loved ones and for those who were injured or suffered economic losses on that "day of infamy" at "ground zero" in New York,[29] at the Pentagon, or in Pennsylvania. However, there have also been nonhumanitarian actions by civilians against other people in the United States (primarily Muslims or people of Middle Eastern or South Asian country ethnic background or citizenship). For example, between September 11 and November 29, 2001, there were a total of 1,441 documented incidents against Muslims living in the United States, including 8 people killed, 265 assaults on or damages to property, and 262 cases of hate mail (CAIR 2001).

One such incident occurred in Pittsburgh on September 19, 2001. On that date, Humair Ahmed, a University of Pittsburgh student from Pakistan, "was punched and beaten by a man who claimed to be enraged by last week's terrorist attacks" (Tinsley 2001, B1). According to a newspaper account published three days later,

> Police said Ahmed told them he was coming home from classes at the University of Pittsburgh ... [when] a man charged at him repeatedly yelling, "Are you from Afghanistan?" Ahmed said he told the man he was Pakistani and tried to walk away, but the man started to kick and punch him. A woman passing by tried to intervene, but the man just pushed her out of the way and attacked again. (Tinsley, 2001, B1)

Ahmed reported to those gathered at a rally for peace held on the campus of the University of Pittsburgh on September 20 that this young woman located someone with a cell phone and called the police. However, the attacker escaped into the nearby construction site, where he was working, and was not taken into custody until he came in to a local police station for questioning on September 21.

Actions undertaken by government officials in the United States also might be perceived to be in violation of the civil liberties (not to mention human rights) of Muslims and people of Middle Eastern and South Asian backgrounds.[30] For instance, as of November 3, 2001, there were approximately 1,150 detainees, what some have labeled

> "disappeared" in the U.S.—people who have been snatched off the streets by agents of the U.S. government, held incommunicado, put in solitary confinement, denied lawyers.... Most of the detained are Saudis and Egyptians. There are also detainees from United Arab Emirates, Yemen, Jordan, Pakistan, India, Morocco, Mauritania and El Salvador. ("Disappeared" 2001, 3)

The legality of such actions has been debated as (a) the initiative by Attorney General John Ashcroft "to have local police interview some 5,000 men and women in

Arab-American and Muslim communities"; (b) the "U.S.A. Patriot Act" (signed in December, 2001); and (c) other U.S. government actions have altered the legal situation with respect to the detention of noncitizens, attorney-client privilege, military tribunals, and rights to privacy (Cohen 2001, 33). Although opinion polls of the American public conducted within four months of the September 11 attacks have shown "strong support for ... detaining legal immigrants[, conducting] ... military tribunals" (Cohen 2001, 30), and "interviewing 5,000 people ...within the Arab-American and Islamic communities" (Stein 2001, 41), civil libertarians in and outside of government have criticized that "some government initiatives aimed at terrorist suspects, like military tribunals, simply go too far[;] ... the new rules may reshape the legal landscape for all Americans[; and] ... the Bush Administration is throwing off the delicate balance among the three branches of government" (Cohen 2001, 32).

An incident that occurred in Pittsburgh on September 20, 2001, gives some indication of how civil liberties, such as freedom of speech, may be being restricted in the United States in the context of the "war on terrorism" (for other incidents in the United States, see Rothschild 2002). On that date, John Gardner was escorted by "four school police officers ... from [the] gymnasium, where he was subbing for the gym teacher, ...was sent home, [and] ... given a formal letter ... [stating that] he was 'released from [his] assignment as a day-to-day substitute teacher with the Pittsburgh Public Schools until further notice'" (Lee 2001, B1). He was dismissed because another teacher had found some notes Gardner scribbled on the edge of a newspaper and gave the "incriminating" evidence to school authorities. The official report stated that Gardner had written the words "'Osama bin Laden did us a favor'" (Lee 2001, B1). In fact, this was part of a longer quote that he heard on a television newscast, which he was watching during his break, and that he thought he might use in a book that he was writing. The quoted material continued, "'He vulcanized us, awakened us and strengthened our resolve'" (Lee 2001, B1). Although Gardner's dismissal was rescinded after he, with the help of the local chapter of the American Civil Liberties Union, filed an appeal, the incident raises concerns about the chilling effect on free speech in the current climate in schools, workplaces, and other settings. Such a climate presents enormous challenges for teaching U.S. educators about issues related to terrorism and Islam.

Conclusion

Educators need to be knowledgeable and encouraged to think critically about topics like "terrorism" and Islam, not only so they can help their students learn about and analyze the related issues. Certainly, the many questions posed about "terrorism" and Islam when we met with a group of fifty-plus doctoral students in Education and with two groups of urban public high school students in the United States indicates the need for preparing teachers to deal with the topics. However, educators also need to be exposed to these topics so that they can make informed decisions about how, if at all, to become involved in the discussions and other actions that are taking place in local, national, and global communities. Our own participation in the Pittsburgh-based "Mobilization for Peace" has reinforced for us the importance of being informed and making choices about what forms of political action and inaction we should pursue.

Our discussion of four national contexts (Egypt, the Philippines, Cuba, and the United States) illustrates the complex challenges that those of us who teach Social Foundations of Education face as we seek to engage preservice and inservice educators on the topics of terrorism and Islam. At the same time, these comparative studies can serve as useful vehicles for facilitating dialogue and reflection among educators in any one society. Oftentimes it is easier to discuss controversial and emotionally laden issues by considering them in a "foreign" and/or a historical context rather than by only seeking to deal with them in one's own contemporary setting. Certainly, taking a comparative approach can enable instructors and students to focus on variations in experience and multiple perspectives, thus deepening and strengthening their critical thinking and action.

Notes

1. For some readers it may be important to note that one of us is a Jewish male professor and U.S. citizen and the other is a Muslim female doctoral student and Egyptian citizen.
2. Historians may be intrigued that Bush's speech was given almost exactly three years following then–U.S. President Bill Clinton' address to the United Nations, on September 21, 1998, at which he "urg[ed] an international front to combat terrorists" (Gellman 2001, 8), this following the bombings of U.S. embassies in Kenya and Tanzania on August 7 of that year.
3. Citing the cases of the Jewish underground in Palestine, the Palestine Liberation Organization, and Osama bin Laden, Ahmad (2002, 47) observes that "terrorists change. The terrorist of yesterday is the hero of today, and the hero of yesterday becomes the terrorist of today."
4. According to Zunes (2001, 3), "Osama bin Laden's key grievances—U.S. support for the Israeli occupation, its ongoing military presence on the Arabian peninsula, the humanitarian consequences of the sanctions against Iraq, and support for corrupt Arab dictatorships—have resonance among the majority of the world's Muslims. Very few Muslims support terrorism of any kind. Yet as long as there is widespread hostility to Washington's Middle East policy, it will not be difficult for terrorists to find willing recruits."
5. In his book, provocatively entitled *Terror in the Mind of God: The Global Rise of Religious Violence,* Juergensmeyer (2000) presents case studies of the ideas and actions of groups that have committed acts of "terrorism" and claim to have done so because they are Buddhists, Catholics, Jews, Muslims, Protestant Christians, or Sikhs. And Gopin (1998, ix) adds Confucianism, Taoism, and Shintoism to this list of religions that have had "periods in which some in their midst utilized repressive religious laws or theological principles to commit unspeakable acts of brutality and terror." For discussions that promote peace and justify violence in Christianity, Islam, and Judaism, respectively, see Hollenbach (1983), Ravitzky (1988), and Al-Faruqi (1981).
6. Note that "[o]ver 1.2 billion people throughout the world are adherents of Islam." (CIE 1995, 2). Furthermore, it is noteworthy that "[w]hile Islam is often associated almost exclusively with the Middle East, Arabs comprise only about 15%–18% of all Muslims(CIE

1995, 2). Finally, it should be noted that "Muslim and Arab are not interchangeable terms. Twelve million Christian and ten thousand Jews live in Arab countries and consider themselves Arab" (AWIR and MEPC 1998, 1).

7. Muslims believe in a series of prophets, from Adam to Muhammad, including Moses and Jesus.

8. Note that women were prohibited from participation in formal education as well as active public roles in the economy and polity under the Taliban regime in Afghanistan. Another interpretation of Islamic law is that women have the right to be educated at a high level, to possess and dispose of property, to undertake a trade or profession, and to vote and serve as government officials (Ali and Ali 2001; AWIR and MEPC 1998; Badawi 1971; Bennoune 1995; El-Saadawi 1995; Ramazani 1995).

9. Interestingly, when on January 19, "the United States military quietly lifted an order ... requiring servicewomen to wear long head scarves and black robes known as *abbayas* when off base" in Saudi Arabia, a decision prompted by a lawsuit filed by "the highest ranking female fighter pilot in the Air Force," at least one American female military officer stated: 'I'm still going to wear the *abbaya* ... I feel more comfortable in it. But I'm sure glad it's my decision now'" (Sciolino 2002, A6).

10. Defining what is or what is not "un-Islamic," of course, is a subjective interpretation, and being un-Islamic is not same as being a non-Muslim.

11. The Muslim Brotherhood's ideas spread to other countries. For instance, the radical Islamic movement in Kabul, Afghanistan, rooted in the 1950s, included students and teachers who had contacts with the Muslim Brotherhood while studying in Egypt (Rubin 1997).

12. Hundreds of Egyptian Muslims participated in the Afghan *jihad* against the Soviet invaders called for by Afghanis pursuing an Islamic state (Chomsky 2001). Rubin (1997) emphasizes that "the Afghan Islamists were connected to an international network that included both Radical Islamists in the Arab world and the U.S. security establishment" (184).

13. *Al-Jama'at al-Islamiyya* is a name of Islamic "fundamentalist" groups in Egypt, which include nonviolent as well as violent groups, such as *al-Takfir wa al-Hegira* (the repentance), *Jama'a Islamiyya* (one Islamic group), and *al-Jihad.*

14. After the 1979 peace accord was signed between Egypt and Israel, and brokered by the United States during the Carter Administration, Egypt has become a major recipient of U.S. aid. During the same time Egypt has been a close ally of the United States, including taking a leading role in securing the cooperation of other Arab states in the U.S.-led "Gulf War" against Iraq, after it had invaded Kuwait in 1990.

15. "A sustained corollary to the government's forceful response has been the use of the state sanctioned 'official' religious establishment as well as the mass media to undermine *al-Jama'at's* claim to Islamic purity" (Tschirgi 1999, 221).

16. Goldberg (2001, 48) illustrates: "Muhammad Atta, who is believed to have flown one of the hijacked planes into the World Trade Center, is the son of a middle-class Cairo lawyer." And Chomsky (2001, 11) indicates further the complexity of the situation, in that Egypt, along with France, Pakistan, Saudi Arabia, and the United States, helped construct "[t]he bin Laden network ... in 1979 ... [drawing] from the most militant sectors they could find, which happened to be radical Islamists, ... to fight a holy war against the Russians" in Afghanistan.

17. In terms of religious identification, Filipinos are 83% Catholic, 9% Protestant, 5% Muslim, and 3% Buddhist and others.

18. Note that the struggle by Muslim groups in the Philippines was not only over political sovereignty, but also over who would control and benefit from economic activity (Milligan 2001).

19. Milligan (2001, 11) observes that education was a major vehicle for combating Muslim Filipino resistance because, although "Islam is generally seen as an impediment to American policy, something to be gotten around, undermined and eventually sidelined," it was necessary for the U.S. occupying force to avoid "any perception of a Spanish-style frontal assault on the faith which would only heighten Muslim Filipino resistance."

20. Milligan (2001, 2) notes that the "13 Islamicized ethno-linguistic groups of the southern Philippines were dubbed 'Moros' by Spanish colonizers in the 16th century after the Muslim 'Moors' of North Africa whom the Spanish had only recently driven from their homeland."

21. According to the Cuban census the population in Cuba is 51% mulatto, 37% White, 11% Black, 1% Chinese (Semester at Sea 1999, 14).

22. Many Cubans identify themselves as atheists or nonbelievers, though the expression of religious beliefs and the practice of religion have increased in recent years. The largest group practice an Afro-Cuban religion, a mixture of African and Catholic traditions similar to Santeria in Brazil, and the largest religious organization is the Catholic Church; there are also Protestants and Jews (Serrano Peralta 2000).

23. The three main arguments for Cuba remaining on the U.S. State Department's list of terrorist nations are identified and then countered in a statement initiated by Wayne Smith, a Cuba specialist at Johns Hopkins and a former State Department officer stationed in Cuba in the 1950s and 1970s: (a) "that Cuba harbors Basque terrorists," (b) "that Cuba has contacts with the Colombian guerrillas and has facilitated meetings between them and the Columbian government," and (c) "that there are a number of fugitives from U.S. justice living in Cuba"; the statement also calls attention to the fact that "there is no credible evidence that any of these groups ... are mounting terrorist actions from Cuba" (Center for International Policy 2001).

24. If one includes structural forms of violence in one's definition of terrorism, then the U.S. embargo on trade with and travel to Cuba could also be considered an act of state terrorism or what the Cuban government calls "merciless economic warfare" (GOC 2001a, 1).

25. Hernández Martínez (1995) describes the diversity of Cuban Americans and their organizations, associated in part with when (pre- or post-1959) and why (political or economic reasons) they and their families migrated to the United States. Moreover, he "argues that the impact of [the anti-Castro] Cuban Americans is not primarily a function of their numerical strength ..., but rather because of their 'belligerance,' their 'economic clout,' their 'advances in legislative and administrative positions at the local level,' and 'especially their practical utility to the U.S. Executive in implementing its policy on Cuba' (e.g., participation in military actions like the Bay of Pigs invasion, managing the U.S. propaganda organs—Radio Marti and TV Marti—directed toward Cuba)" (summarized in Ginsburg et al. 1997, xii).

26. U.S.-born converts to Islam include white and especially black non-Hispanics, but also a growing group of Hispanics (Wakin 2002).

27. "The United States Department of Defense reports that there are currently more than 9,000 Muslims on active duty in the U.S. armed services. A number of leading American scientists, physicians, sports figures, and scholars are Muslim" (CIE 1995, 4).

28. Adding to the complexity of understanding the purposes (or consequences) of development aid, "U.S. Treasury officials estimate that for every $1.00 the United States lends, [U.S.-based companies] get back $2.00 in bank-financed procurement contracts ... [because] poor countries receiving the loans are forced to buy products from [the U.S.]" (Braun 1997, 68).

29. There has been some debate whether the events of September 11, 2001, can be equated with those of December 7, 1941, which then President Franklin Delano Roosevelt termed a "day of infamy." However, we are surprised—and disturbed—that few, if any, questions have been raised about the use of the label "ground zero" for the former site of the World Trade Center in New York City, and thus seemingly equating the recent tragedy with devastation of life and property at "ground zero" in Hiroshima, Japan, when "217,137 people were killed, including an estimated 140,000 who had died [by the end of 1945] as a direct result of the [U.S. atomic] bombing" on August 6, 1945 (F2/network 2000).

30. It is instructive to note, as Gage (2001, 17) did several months before September 11, "After [the] McCarran-Walter [law] was finally abolished in 1994, it was quickly supplanted by the Antiterrorism and Effective Death Penalty Act (AEDPA) signed in 1996. Anti-communism was replaced with anti-terrorism.... People—largely Arabs and Muslims—have been held in jail for up to 4 years, denied bond using evidence they and their lawyers cannot see. In almost every case, when the individuals are arrested, the government

calls them terrorists and claims they have committed heinous acts. But rather than charge them with these crimes, the government instead tries to deport them."

References

"After the Attack ... The War on Terrorism." 2001. *Monthly Review* 53 (6): 1–9.

Ahmad, Eqbal. 2002. "Straight Talk on Terrorism." *Monthly Review* 53 (January): 46–54.

Al-Faruqi, Ismail. 1981. "Introduction." Pp. xiii–xxiv in *The Islamic Theory of International Relations.* Edited by Abdul-Hamid Abdul-Sulayman. New York: The International Institute of Islamic Thought.

Ali, Amir. 2001. "Jihad Explained." Retrieved December 22, 2001, from http://thetruereligion.org/jihad.htm

Ali, Mary. 2001. "The Question of Hijab: Suppression or Liberation?" Chicago: The Institute of Islamic Information and Education. Retrieved on December 22, 2001, from http://www.usc.edu/dept/MSA/humanrelations/womeninislam/whatishijab.html

Ali, Mary, and Anjum Ali. 2001. "Women's Liberation through Islam." Chicago: The Institute of Islamic Information and Education. Retrieved on December 22, 2001, from http://thetruereligion.org/womenslib.htm

Al-Mashat, R., and D. Grigorian. 1998. *Economic Reforms in Egypt: Emerging Patterns and Their Possible Implications.* Washington, D.C.: World Bank.

Amnesty International. 1998. "The United States of America: Rights for All" (especially chaps. 1, 7, and 8). London: Amnesty International. Retrieved on December 22, 2001, from http://web.amnesty.org/ai.nsf/Index/AMR510351998?OpenDocument&of=COUNTRI ES\USA

Arab World and Islamic Resources (AWIR) and Middle East Policy Council (MEPC). 1998. *The Arab World Studies Notebook.* Berkeley, Calif.: A Joint Publication of: AWIR and Middle East Policy Council.

Arkoun, Mohammed, and Udo Steinbach. 2000. "Foreword." Pp. xi–xvi in *The Islamic World and the West: An Introduction to Political Cultures and International Relations.* Edited by Kai Hafez. Translated by M. Kenny. Boston, Leiden, Köln: Brill.

Badawi, Jamal. 1971. "The Status of Women in Islam." *Al-Ijtihad* 8 (2): 17–21.

Barber, Benjamin. 2001. "Jihad vs. McWorld." Pp. 21–27 in *The Globalization Reader.* Edited by F. Lechner and J. Boli. Oxford, England: Blackwell Publishers.

Bennoune, Karima. 1995. "Islamic Fundamentalism Represses Women." Pp. 64–71 in *Islam: Opposing Viewpoints.* Edited by D. Bender and B. Leone. San Diego: Greenhaven Press.

Braun, Denny. 1997. *The Rich Get Richer: The Rise of Income Inequality in the United States and the World.* 2nd ed. Chicago: Nelson-Hall.

Brock-Utne, Birgit. 1989. *Feminist Perspectives on Peace and Peace Education.* New York: Pergamon.

Burbules, Nicholas, and Carlos Alberto Torres, eds. 2000. *Education and Globalization: Critical Perspectives.* New York: Routledge.

Center for International Policy. 2001. "Cuba Policy Should be Reviewed in New International Context." Retrieved on December 15, 2001, from http://www.ciponline.org/cuba/newsarticles/pressrelease092501.htm

Chand, Attar. 1992. *Islam and the New World Order.* New Delhi: Akashdeep Publishing House.

Chomsky, Noam. 2001. "The United States is a Leading Terrorist State: An Interview by David Baramian." *Monthly Review* 53 (6): 10–19.

Cohen, Adam. 2001. "Rough Justice." *Time,* December 10, 30–38.

Cook, Bradly. 2001. "Islam and Egyptian Higher Education: Student Attitudes." *Comparative Education Review* 45 (3): 339–411.

Council on American-Islamic Relations (CAIR). 2001. Retrieved on January 3, 2002, from http://www.cair-net.org/asp/aboutislam.asp

Council on Islamic Education (CIE). 1995. *Teaching About Islam and Muslims in the Public School Classroom.* 3rd ed. Fountain Valley, Calif.: CIE Publications.

Cullison, Alan, and Andrew Higgins. 2002. "Al-Qaida File Maps Attack-Scouting Trip to Israel, Egypt." *Pittsburgh Post-Gazette,* January 17, A5.

Danskin, Edith. 1979. Quality and Quantity in Higher Education in Thailand and Philippines. *Comparative Education* 15 (3): 313–321.

Dao, James, and Eric Schmitt. 2002. "Next U.S. Targets May Be Terrorists in Lawless Areas." *New York Times,* January 8, A1, A18.

"Disappeared in the USA." 2001. *Revolutionary Worker* (November 11): 3, 14.

Doi, Abdur-Rahman. 2001. "Modesty." Retrieved on December 29, 2001, from http://www.usc.edu/dept/MSA/humanrelations/womeninislam/womeninsociety.html

Domhoff, G. William. 1998. "Power and Class in the United States." Pp. 1–32 in *Who Rules America: Power and Politics in the Year 2000.* 3rd ed. Mountain View, Calif.: Mayfield Publishing.

Domínguez García María Isabel. 1997. "Generations and Participation in Cuba." Pp. 1–12 in *Cuba in the Special Period: Cuban Perspectives.* Edited by Frank McGlynn, Mark Ginsburg, Jose Moreno, and Niurka Pérez Rojas. Williamsburg, Va.: Studies in Third World Societies (Number 60).

Dorgan, Michael. 2001. "Mindanao in Philippines May Be Next U.S. Target." *Pittsburgh Post-Gazette,* December 27, A27.

Dunn, Michael. 1995. "The Islamic Revolution Is Not Taking Root in Egypt." Pp. 268–276 in *Islam: Opposing Viewpoints.* Edited by D. Bender and B. Leone. San Diego: Greenhaven Press.

El-Saadawi, Nawal. (1995). "Women Should Reject Islamic Gender Roles: An Interview by Gorge Lerner." Pp. 80–88 in *Islam: Opposing Viewpoints.* Edited by D. Bender and B. Leone. San Diego: Greenhaven Press.

Federal Research Division. 1990. "Egypt—A Country Study." Library of Congress. Retrieved on January 8, 2002, http://lcwb2.loc.gov/frd/cs/egypt/eg_appen.html

F2/network. 2000. "Thousands Remember at Hiroshima's Ground Zero." Retrieved on January 11, 2001, from http://www.theage.com.au/news/20000807/A53134-2000Aug6.html

FORSNET. 2000. "Middle East and Terrorism: Islamic Group and War (Egypt)." Retrieved on January 20, 2002, from http://www.teror.gen.tr/english/middleeast/organisations/radical/islamicgroup.html

Frontline. 2001. "Osama bin Laden v. the U.S.: Edicts and Statements." Retrieved on January 5, 2002, from http://www.pbs.org/wgbh/pages/frontline/shows/binladen/who/edicts/html

Funk and Wagnalls Standard Dictionary. 1980. New York: Signet.

Gage, Kit. 2001. "Demonizing Dissent." *Independent Politics News* (Spring): 17.

Galtung, Johan. 1969. "Violence, Peace and Peace Research." *Journal of Peace Research* 6:167–191.

Garver, Newton. 1968. "What is Violence?" *The Nation* 206:819.

Gellman, Barton. 2001. "Clinton's Covert War: The U.S. Targeted bin Laden for Years But Shied Away from a Direct Hit." *The Washington Post National Weekly Edition,* January 7–13, 6–8.

Ginsburg, Mark, ed. 1995. *Politics of Educators' Work and Lives.* New York: Garland.

Ginsburg, Mark, with Thomas Clayton, Michel Rakotomanana, and Gilda Holly. 1998. "Education for All or Educating All for Peace." Pp. 233–297 in *Lifelong Education for All.* Edited by Shen-Keng Yang. Taipei: Chinese Comparative Education Society—Tapei.

Ginsburg, Mark, and Beverly Lindsay, eds. 1995. *The Political Dimension in Teacher Education: Comparative Perspectives on Policy Formation, Socialization and Society.* New York: Falmer.

Ginsburg, Mark, Frank McGlynn, Jose Moreno, and Niurka Pérez Rojas. 1997. "Political Economic Challenges and Responses within the State and Civil Society in Cuba." Pp. ix–xxvi in *Cuba in the Special Period: Cuban Perspectives.* Edited by Frank McGlynn,

Mark Ginsburg, Jose Moreno, and Niurka Pérez Rojas. Williamsburg, Va.: Studies in Third World Societies (Number 60).

Giroux, Henry. 1997. *Pedagogy and the Politics of Hope: Theory, Culture and Schooling: A Critical Reader.* Boulder, Colo.: Westview Press.

Gitlin, Todd. 2002. "Blaming America First." *Mother Jones,* January-February, 22–25.

Glaberson, William. 2001. "Interpreting Law for American Muslims." *New York Times,* October 21, A18.

Goldberg, Jeffrey. 2001. "Behind Mubarak: Egyptian Clerics and Intellectuals Respond to Terrorism." *The New Yorker,* October 8, 48–55.

Golden, Tim. 1998 (13 September). "After Lift of a Papal Visit, the Cuban Church Has a Letdown." *New York Times.* Retrieved on December 15, 2001, from http://www.nytimes.com/library/world/americas/091398cuba-catholics.html

Gopin, Marc. 1998. "Foreword." Pp. vii–xi in *The Future of Islam and the West: Clash of Civilizations or Peaceful Coexistence?* Edited by S. Hunter. Washington, D.C.: Center for Strategic and International Studies.

Government of Cuba (GOC). 2001a. *Cuba's Report to the Secretary General of the United Nations Organization on Resolution 55/20 of UN's General Assembly.* (November).

———. 2001b. *Statement of the Government of the Republic of Cuba.* (September 11): 1.

Grundy, Kenneth, and Michael Weinstein. 1974. *The Ideologies of Violence.* Columbus, Ohio: Charles E. Merrill.

Gutek, Gerald.1997. *American Education in a Global Society.* Prospect Heights, Ill.: Waveland Press.

Herman, Edward. 1982. *The Real Terror Network: Terrorism in Fact and Propaganda.* Boston: South End Press.

Hernández Martínez, Jorge. 1997. "The Cuban Community, Political Power and the United States' Plans regarding Cuba." Pp. 67–76 in *Cuba in the Special Period: Cuban Perspectives.* Edited by Frank McGlynn, Mark Ginsburg, Jose Moreno, and Niurka Pérez Rojas. Williamsburg, Va.: Studies in Third World Societies (Number 60).

Hollenbach, David. 1983. "The Relation of Justice and Peace." Pp. 16–24 in *Nuclear Ethics: A Christian Moral Argument.* Ramsey, N.J.: Paulist Press.

Hunter, Shireen. 1998. *The Future of Islam and the West: Clash of Civilizations or Peaceful Coexistence?* Washington, D.C.: Center for Strategic and International Studies.

Ibrahim, Ibrahim. 1987. "Religion and Politics Under Nasser and Sadat, 1952–1981." Pp. 121–134 in *The Islamic Impulse.* Edited by B. Stowasser. London: Croom Helm.

Islam Today. Retrieved on December 28, 2001, from http://www.islamtoday.net

Islamic Institute. "Understanding Islam and the Muslims." Retrieved on December 28, 2001, from http://www.islamicinstitute.org/understanding.htm

Joan, Sumayyah. 1999 (December). "Hijab." *Resala.* Retrieved on December 28, 2001, from http://thetruereligion.org/hijabjoan.htm.

Juergensmeyer, Mark. 1995. "The Islamic Revolution Is Taking Root in Egypt." Pp. 259–267 in *Islam: Opposing Viewpoints.* Edited by D. Bender and B. Leone. San Diego: Greenhaven Press.

———. 2000. *Terror in the Mind of God: The Global Rise of Religious Violence.* Berkeley: University of California Press.

Kahn, Joseph. 2001. "A Trend Toward Attacks that Emphasize Deaths." *New York Times,* September 12, A18.

Kanpol, Barry. 1999. *Critical Pedagogy: An Introduction.* 2nd ed. Westport, Conn.: Bergen & Garvey.

Kawell, Joann. 2001. "Terror's Latin American Profile." *NACLA Report on the Americas* 35 (3): 50–53.

Kohli, Wendi. 2002/this issue. "Situated Knowing: Mind, Body, and Soul: Presidential Address." *Educational Studies* 33:261–277.

Lacayo, Richard. 2001. "About Face: An Inside Look at How Women Fared under Taliban Oppression and What the Future Holds for Them Now." *Time,* December 3, 34–49.

Landau, Anya, and Wayne Smith. November 2001. "Keeping Things in Perspective: Cuba and the Question of Terrorism." Retrieved on December 14, 2001, from http://ciponline.org/Cuba/main/keepingthingsinperspective.htm.

Lee, Carmen. 2001. "Sub Teacher Fired Over bin Laden Note." *Pittsburgh Post-Gazette,* September 21, B1.

Lewis, Anthony. 2001. "A Different World." *New York Times,* September 12, A27.

Luke, Carmen, and Jennifer Gore. 1992. *Feminisms and Critical Pedagogy.* New York: Routledge.

Marger, Martin. 1997. "Ethnic Stratification: Power and Inequality." Pp. 37–69 in *Race and Ethnic Relations: American and Global Perspectives.* Belmont, Calif.: Wadsworth.

Marvel, Bill, and Aline McKenzie. 2001. "Our Lives Will Divide into Before and After." *Pittsburgh Post-Gazette,* September 12, A5.

McClintock, Michael. 1991. "American Doctrine and Counterinsurgent State Terror." Pp. 123–138 in *Western State Terrorism.* Edited by Alexander George. New York: Routledge.

McSherry, J. Patrice. 2002. "Tracking the Origins of a State Terror Network: Operation Condor." *Latin American Perspectives* 29 (1): 38–60.

Miller, Tom. 1996. *Trading with the Enemy: A Yankee Travels through Castro's Cuba.* New York: Basic Books.

Milligan, Jeffrey Ayala. 2001. "The American Education of Muslim Filipinos, 1898–1920." Paper presented at the annual meeting of the American Educational Studies Association. Miami, Florida. October 31–November 4.

Perez, Louis. 1998. *The War of 1898: The United States and Cuba in History and Historiography.* Chapel Hill: University of North Carolina Press.

Pinn, Irmgard. 2000. "From Exotic Harem Beauty to Islamic Fundamentalist: Women in Islam." Pp. 57–69 in *The Islamic World and the West: An Introduction to Political Cultures and International Relations.* Edited by K. Hafez. Translated by M. Kenny. Boston: Brill

Pressley, Sue Anne. 2002. "Captives Arrive at Base in Cuba." *Pittsburgh Post-Gazette,* January 12, A1, A14.

Ramazi, Nesta. 1995. "Islamic Government Need Not Repress Women." Pp. 72–79 in *Islam: Opposing Viewpoints.* Edited by D. Bender and B. Leone. San Diego: Greenhaven Press.

Ravitzky, Aviezer. 1988. "Peace." Pp. 685–702 in *Contemporary Jewish Religious Thought.* Edited by A. Cohen and P. Mendez-Flohr. New York: Free Press.

Rius. 1970. *Cuba for Beginners: An Illustrated Guide for Americans (and Their Government) to Socialist Cuba.* New York: Pathfinder Press.

Robinson, Linda. 1998. "What Didn't We Do to Get Rid of Castro? Declassified Documents Tell More Tales." *U.S. News and World Report,* October 26, 26.

Rothschild, Matthew. 2002. "The New McCarthyism." *The Progressive* (January): 18–23.

Rubin, Barnett. 1997. "Arab Islamist in Afghanistan." Pp. 179–206 in *Political Islam: Revolution, Radicalism, or Reform?* Edited by J. Eposito. London: Lynne Rienner Publishers.

Sanford, Nevitt. 1971. "Collective Destructiveness: Sources and Remedies." Pp. 25–38 in *Perspectives on Violence.* Edited by Gene Usdin. New York: Brunner/Mazel.

Schmitt, Eric. 2002. "U.S. and Philippines Setting Up Joint Command to Combat Terror." *New York Times,* January 16, A1, A11.

Sciolino, Elaine. 2002. "Servicewomen Win, Doffing their Veils in Saudi Arabia." *New York Times,* January 25, A6.

Semester at Sea. 1999. *Global Perspectives: World Regional Geography.* Sluice Dock, Conn.: Dushkin/McGraw-Hill.

Serrano Peralta, Lourdes. 1995. "Estructura y Relaciones Raciales en un Barrio Popular: Mujeres, Instrucción, Occupación, y Color de la Piel [Structure and Race Relations in a Neighborhood: Women, Education, Occupation, and Skin Color]." Paper presented at the Post-LASA Conference on *Public Policy Challenges and Social Diversity in Cuba.* University of Pittsburgh, October 1–3.

————. 2000. "Religious Currents in the Caribbean." Presentation at the conference on *Cuba and/in the Caribbean*. University of Pittsburgh, Pennsylvania, October 24–26.

Sluka, Jeffrey. 2000. "Introduction." Pp. 1–13 in *Death Squad: The Anthropology of State Terror*. Edited by J. Sluka. Philadelphia: University of Pennsylvania Press.

Spiegel, John. 1971. "Toward a Theory of Collective Violence." Pp. 83–96 in *Dynamics of Violence*. Edited by Jan Fawcett. Chicago: American Medical Association.

Stein, Joel. 2001. "Just a Few Questions." *Time*, December 10, 41.

Stromquist, Nelli, and Karen Monkman, eds. 2000. *Globalization and Education: Integration and Contestation Across Cultures*. Lanham, Md.: Rowan and Littlefield.

Tinsley, M. Ferguson. 2001. "Pakistani Student Attacked Near Pitt." *Pittsburgh Post-Gazette*, September 22, B1.

Tschirgi, Dan. 1999. "Marginalized Violent Internal Conflict in the Age of Globalization: Mexico and Egypt." Pp. 217–242 in *Globalization: Polices, Challenges, and Responses*. Edited by S. Ismael. Calgary, Alberta, Canada: Detselig Enterprises Ltd.

Vogel, Steve. 2002. "U.S. Troops to Fight Philippine Guerrillas." *Pittsburgh Post-Gazette*, January 16, A8.

Voll, John. 1994. *Islam: Continuity and Change in the Modern World*. 2nd ed. New York: Syracuse University Press.

Wakin, Daniel. 2002. "Growing Number of Latino-Americans Turn to Islam." *New York Times*, January 2, A16.

Webster's New Collegiate Dictionary. 1961. Springfield, Mass.: G. & C. Merriam Company.

World Book 2001 CD, U.S. Census 1990.

Zuhur, Sherifa. 1995. "Women Can Embrace Islamic Gender Roles." Pp. 89–97 in *Islam: Opposing Viewpoints*. Edited by D. Bender and B. Leone. San Diego: Greenhaven Press.

Zunes, Stephen. 2001. "International Terrorism." *Foreign Policy in Focus* 3 (38): 1–3.

Correspondence should be addressed to Mark Ginsburg and Nagwa Megahed, University of Pittsburgh/IISE-School of Education, SKO1 Forbes Quad, Pittsburgh, PA 15260. E-mail: mbg@pitt.edu or nmmst19@pitt.edu

---

Brutal Compassion: A Requiem

DONNA ADAIR BREAULT
Illinois State University

Requiem Aeternum[1]

The smoke lingers over Manhattan as the nation stirs from its shock. Many cling to common national symbols—a forgotten sense of patriotism. They welcome the military intervention and follow it carefully on the news, for it offers the appearance of control in these uncertain times. Others wrap their disequilibrium around them like a blanket, afraid to explore the questions that hover at a distance. The nation pauses for a moment—stunned, numb.

Dies Irae²

There is nothing beautiful left in the streets of this city.
I have come to believe in death and renewal by fire.
Past questioning the necessities of blood
why it must be mine or my children's time
that will see this grim city quake to be reborn perhaps
blackened again but this time with a sense of purpose. (emphasis added; Lorde
1992c, 135)

How do we live with our rage for the rank consumption and economic gluttony, for the power of the few over the many, for all that the Twin Towers symbolized, while honoring the utter emotional disembodiment we feel for the human loss within our nation? How do we support patriotic notions when we see what our nation's power has done to others around the world? How can we reconcile the fact that the police who are now touted as heroes were, merely decades ago, called "pigs"? Can we hold on to the beliefs that caused us to call some police pigs years ago and yet still honor their bravery and mourn for their loss? How can we read the lines of Audre Lorde's poem "New York City" and attempt to understand the harsh judgments she levied on those in power;

They think they are praying when they squat
to shit money-pebbles shaped like their parents' brains—
who exist to go into dust to exist again
grosser and more swollen
and without ever relinquishing space
or breath or energy from their private hoard. (Lorde 1992c, 137)

Are these not the people who are now victims in the Twin Towers attack? Can we simultaneously feel the pain of a wretched African American woman, raising her children in a city that did not keep the promises it made during the civil rights movement, and yet at the same time mourn for the White upper-middle-class mother who now has to raise her children alone? If we can manage this, can we also recognize that the collective existence of those upper-middle-class individuals perpetuates the unjust conditions in which the poor of New York must live? As intellectuals, it is easy to view the world through a critical lens, yet when that lens cannot acknowledge the moral complexity of our world, we find ourselves ideologically impotent.

Offertorium

> *I submit them*
> *Loving them above all others save myself*
> *To the fire to the rage to the ritual sacrifications*
> *To be tried as new steel is tried.* (emphasis added; Lorde 1992c, 136)

Art, since ancient times, has portrayed the human spirit in a mediated sense. In this manner, one can find parallels between art and theorizing. Although artistic mediums vary, the complexity of the human spirit, its multidimensionality and its contradictions, is difficult if not impossible to accurately portray. For example, in his fresco *The Massacre of the Innocents,* Giotto recounts the slaughter of infant boys in Egypt. Emotion is absent from the faces of the murderers, and the appeals from the mothers appear as emotionally distant as the pile of dead infants in the center of the scene. Similarly, in his painting *Thief on a Cross,* Campin depicts a crucifixion, perhaps one of the most brutal of acts, as a peaceful and noble transition from life to death. Such renderings are not relegated to religious scenes alone. In David's 1793 painting *The Death of Marat,* the painter chooses to portray the murdered French hero lying peacefully in his bathtub. In his painting, the hero who had suffered from skin disease and who had been constantly plagued by scabs and boils lies in his bathtub with perfectly white skin—cleansed through death.

Scenes of war also offer mediated versions of our collective human spirit. Consider Goya's painting detailing the Spanish slaughter of 1808, *The Third of May, 1808.* In Goya's painting, Spanish patriots climb a hill only to encounter a firing squad and certain death. The primary subject of the painting stands and faces the firing squad. While other men on the hill cower and cover their faces, this man stands, arms outstretched, offering his life for his country with little emotion revealed. As he stands there, a light shines upon him as if to honor his sacrifice. Goya's portrayal, while honoring what happened on that day in May, allows the viewer to acknowledge the brutality in a mediated sense. You can see it without feeling it. The painting does not leave you with a disturbed sense of a collective self. Soldiers go to war, and soldiers die. Dying for their countries makes them heroes. The act offers some sense of redemption.

In contrast, Picasso's painting *Guernica* reveals the brutal bombing of citizens in that city without affording any sense of compassion. Like Goya, Picasso offers a figure facing death with outstretched hands, but there is no peace within the figure's face—no redemption within the scene. Picasso manages to capture the complex emotions of terror in the faces of his mutilated figures. In doing so, he moves the scene beyond lore to acknowledge the pain and horror of the event. Unlike Goya's representation of war, you cannot leave Picasso's painting unchanged. You carry his images with you within the depths of your soul, forever trying to reconcile the ugliness with your beliefs about the promise of the human spirit. Yet, with its vivid depiction of the brutality of the bombing, Picasso cannot also acknowledge other dimensions of the human spirit: compassion, honor, and dignity, among others. The only sign of hope is one small flower in the hand of the slain soldier, and that he carries with his sword.

To what degree do we as theorists, philosophers, and educators operate within a mediated sense of reality? Do we filter the complex worlds around us through our ideologies only to become passive toward the actual pain of mankind? Can we see only one dimension within our theorizing, one direction of thought? What do we do with those ideas that contradict our own beliefs? Do we recognize those around us whose values differ from our own? As a result of our mediated existences, do we then offer our students empty ideas founded upon abstracted realities? If so, what are our students to do with these empty ideas? Dare we attempt to capture within our theorizing that which escapes capture on the canvas? And what can we expect if we do not find space for the beautiful and the ugly, the honorable and the vile?

Quid Sum Miser[3]

> *"What the eyes don't see, the heart doesn't hurt."* (emphasis added; Lorde 1992a, 134)

How can we see the vile in the midst of the honorable? How do we create images that accurately portray not only the heroics and the loss but the ugliness as well? How do we create these disturbing images and then live with them as our constant companions? Although we are conditioned but not predetermined, we must nevertheless acknowledge and accept responsibility for our conditioned-ness. We build our faith in the human spirit with all that is noble, honorable, and beautiful in our collective lives. We look to what is possible and feel good about who we are. But what if we started with the ugly and vile that bring us together? What if we were to gaze upon the most wretched of common denominators in our midst? As painful as that would be, would we not gain some greater sense of understanding of our responsibilities within the world?

A collective effort of this magnitude would require us to come together exposed, vulnerable, and fully engaged in the pain around us. We would have to acknowledge our role in creating such pain—however far removed our complicity may appear at the surface. We would have to reject the ideas and beliefs that create and sustain opportunities for our insularity and embrace the magnitude of our "conjugating business" (Lorde 1992b, 20) by seeing the world, both the beautiful and the hideous, and by seeing our place in that world.

As things return to normal on Wall Street, we must heed Marley's cry from Dickens's *A Christmas Carol*. Mankind is our business. Human welfare is our business. The chains we forge in life with our ideas, arguments, and academic treatises are just as confining and just as insidious as Scrooge's chains of ledgers and cash boxes. To what degree in our academic lives do we stray no farther than our own ivory towers—while the world waits and hurts, while the naïve hope? Like Scrooge, we should fear both ignorance and want—but ignorance most of all. For it is ignorance that confuses patriotism with colonialism; it is ignorance that sacrifices civil liberties; and it is ignorance that creates racial, ethnic, and religious persecution in a country founded upon difference.

Sanctus[4]

> *What does the we-bird see with*
> *who has lost its I's?* (emphasis added; Lorde 1992a, 134)

Where are we to find peace while the smoke lingers in the midst of the ruins? How do we reconcile all that we have professed through the years? Our beliefs are tested just as the steel of the Twin Towers was tested. Where is hope for the future when the present looks so dark? The conundrum would not be so vexing if it was merely a matter of situating ourselves within our newly shattered world. But no, we have responsibilities to those whom we teach. We must wrestle with these issues while we continue to guide and support our students. We cannot offer them the emptiness we feel right now.

The only way we can reconcile the vile and the noble is to fully embrace each. We must create a space within our selves as well as within our collective bodies where the pain of others and the complexity surrounding their pain can exist indefinitely. Otherwise we will retreat into ideological and moral passivity. We will continue to offer ideas without significance to our students and send them out into the schools without a conviction to engage fully within their daily realities. As Sennett argues, we must create and sustain a disturbed sense of self. We must recognize the pain of others; we must consciously explore the complexity of that pain, and we must understand that there is no easy remedy for it. He notes,

> This can only occur, I believe, by understanding why bodily pain requires a place in which it can be acknowledged, and in which its transcendent origins become visible. Such a pain has a trajectory in human experience ... the body accepting pain is ready to become a civic body.... But the body can follow this civic trajectory only if it acknowledges that there is no remedy for its sufferings in the contrivings of society, that its unhappiness has come from elsewhere, that is pain derives from God's command to live together as exiles. (Sennett 1994, 376)

Pain becomes a transcendent force when we come together as vulnerable yet equal beings and create a space that recognizes and honors all that make us a civic body—the honorable, the vile, as well as the mundane. Only then can we work together to esteem something greater than ourselves. Only then can we fulfill both our professional and our moral responsibilities within the world.

Stabat Mater[5]

> *I walk down the withering limbs*
> *Of New York my last discarded house*
> *And there is nothing worth salvage left in this city*
> *But faint reedy voices like echoes*
> *Of once beautiful children.* (emphasis added; Lorde 1992c, 137)

As theorists, we need to seek a maternal sense of our collective self in order to create space for brutal compassion. Lorde offers three maternal images that explore the difficulties we face in such endeavors. First, she offers an image of promise. An inner-city teacher shares stories with her children at lunchtime. At a time in their lives when " ... what we need and do not have / deadens us / and promises sound like destruction," (Lorde 1992d, 102) the teacher gives her children stories of hope. All the while this teacher knows the odds are against them. She knows the statistics of how many of her boys may end up dead or in prison before they reach adulthood. She knows the likelihood that her girls will have children as children. She knows how difficult it will be for these children to escape their likely futures. Nevertheless, she persists. Ultimately she concludes, "who will say / Promise corrupts / what it does not invent?"(Lorde 1992d, 103).

Lorde's second maternal image is one of despair. In this poem, a child excitedly shows her mother a seed given to her by the strawmen. She appeals to her mother. The strawmen left no tools with which the child could plant the seed, and her world is covered in snow and ice. Nevertheless, the girl pleads to plant the seed and dreams of the possibilities that might sprout from it. In response, the mother beats the child until she accepts the reality of her icy surroundings and rejects the possibilities afforded by the one seed. The mother responds to her daughter, "I don't fatten frogs to feed snakes" (Lorde 1992a, 134).

A final image Lorde offers speaks more broadly to motherhood itself. In this poem, a young girl, a junkie, sits beside a woman on the subway and drifts off to sleep. The woman sees the failure of this girl as if it reflects her own maternal inadequacies—as the failure of all mothers. Offering the girl help, the woman is met with loud laughter. Up and down the aisle of the subway car, mothers look away—afraid to see the unrealized dreams for their own children in the form of this junkie (Lorde 1992e).

How do we achieve a maternal sense of our collective selves? We must engage ourselves, fully committed, in a permanent relationship with our world and all it holds. We must cleave to our collective bosom the liberating and the oppressive, the honorable and the vile, and we must acknowledge that it is all part of us. Like Lorde's teacher, we must persist even though we know the odds for society are bleak. We must not avert our eyes when we witness failure. Although we are "elementary forces colliding in free fall" (Lorde 1992d, 102), we still have control over our commitment to the world with all of its disappointments and its possibilities. Most important, as teachers of teachers, we must not fatten frogs to feed snakes. We must not offer our students isolated ideas abstracted from their realities. We must expose ourselves, our unfinished-ness, our unsettled-ness. We must create within our classrooms space for vulnerability and for confusion. Within that space, a seed can be planted that will bring forth the new sense of compassion needed in our world today.

Notes

1. "Rest Eternal."
2. "Day of Wrath."
3. "What Affliction."
4. "Sanctuary."
5. "Sorrowful Mother."

References

Lorde, Audre.1992a. "Ballad From Childhood." P. 134 in *Undersong*. New York: Norton.
———.1992b. "Bloodbirth." Pp. 19–20 in *Undersong*. New York: Norton.
———. 1992c. "New York City." Pp. 135–137 in *Undersong*. New York: Norton.
———.1992d. "Teacher." Pp. 102–103 in *Undersong*. New York: Norton.
———.1992e. "To My Daughter The Junkie on the Train." Pp. 144–145 in *Undersong*. New York: Norton.
Sennett, Richard. 1994. *Flesh and Stone: The Body and the City in Western Civilization*. New York: Norton.

Correspondence should be addressed to Donna Adair Breault, Illinois State University, 232 DeGarmo Hall, Campus Box 5300, Normal, IL 61790–5330.

THE SOCIAL FOUNDATIONS CLASSROOM

Cracks in the Mirror: Education in a Fractured World

JAYLYNNE N. HUTCHINSON
Ohio University

In the wake of the responses to the tragedy of September 11, I argue that it is not just our world that was fractured but our own worldviews that mirror back to us what we see. Rather than perceiving this fracturing of our worldviews as a negative occurrence, I argue that the fracturing is a necessary step for critical and progressive educators to disrupt the ordinariness and often distorted reflections of life to which we become accustomed.

Like so many others, I watched in horror and disbelief that morning in September as the news show I was watching displayed what the broadcasters had not even understood at first. I was getting ready for work, getting ready to teach a group of sophomore preservice teachers in an educational partnership focused on democratic education. It was only the second week of the quarter. The students were just beginning the democratic education program and were starting to get the hint that education was a political endeavor. For a moment I thought of canceling the class but then realized that many of my students who were already on campus might not have even heard about the events that were unfolding. Although part of me wanted simply wanted to stay glued to the television coverage, I knew that it would be important for me to meet my students.

That was a good choice. It was true—only about one-third of the class had heard the news. I told them what I knew at this point and then asked the members of the class who knew of the events to share their understandings. We were numb, confused, afraid without knowing why. At first I was frustrated that the television in the room didn't connect to outside coverage, but I soon appreciated the fact that we began to dialogue about the events. The discussion would thread throughout the rest of the quarter. The series of events that are even now ongoing have provided a new perspective on liberatory democratic education and have helped me see that we must have the courage to face ourselves in the mirror, even if it cracks. And perhaps, cracking would be the best thing to happen.

The social mirrors that surround us too often reflect the constructions by which we have been conditioned to see and interpret our world. The mirror is not necessarily a good thing unless we are willing to see it crack ... split wide open and spill out the social constructions that insulate and protect us from interfacing with others different from ourselves. Rather than providing us with expanded views of ourselves and the world, the mirror too often reflects back masks of mystification. In fact, this event has given me a new appreciation of the many different types of mirrors in the funhouse. I used to think that the funhouse mirrors were distortions of reality, but now I wonder why I ever thought that a "real" mirror was more likely to provide better information. Adrienne Rich once made a piercing observation. She said, "When someone with the authority of a teacher, say, describes the world and you are not in it, there is a moment of psychic disequilibrium, as if you looked into a mirror and saw nothing" (1989, ix). I would like to expand Rich's notion here and posit that not only are the moments when we look into mirrors and do not see ourselves unsettling, but there are moments when funhouse mirrors are held up to us and we want to turn away from what we see. It is too disconcerting. 9/11 was one of those times.

Hence, as an educator I find even greater evidence of the need for critical democratic education. I can speak only to the U.S. context, but this I know: There is great resistance to look at ourselves in mirrors other than those we have carefully crafted, as individuals, families, and societies. Many times throughout the rest of the quarter, I would be reminded of this resistance. It was as if we feared that by looking at ourselves we would somehow negate our grief over the horrific tragedy and loss of life. How clearly this demonstrates our traditional thinking. Rather than being able to hold within our own minds and hearts the paradox presented to us by this situation, we seem to clutch for those things that will allow us to make sense of the events in as "black and white" a manner as possible. Many students, faculty, and community members had difficulty conceiving that looking at ourselves with different lenses and grieving for the tremendous loss could be done simultaneously. Looking at our role on the world stage was not an attempt to blame ourselves or justify the horrific act of terrorism.

Those advocating a peace-based solution were in a small minority. From my vantage point, those advocating a peace-based solution after the tragedy were attempting to engage in multiple levels of reasoning and feeling about the situation and were asking us to consider how U.S. policies impact the rest of the world. They were attempting to make sense of both the grief and horror of the tragedy and their belief that many of the political and economic policies of the United States contributed to the unfolding of the events. The mirror had fractured for them as well, and they were working to understand the different images reflected back to them.

Attempting to go beyond the political and mainstream media rhetoric of "these Islamic fundamentalists simply hate the freedom and democracy that the United States represents" was a difficult task. It was difficult because any attempt at articulating another worldview was most often dismissed with the rightest rhetorical descriptors of "commie liberals," "dirty hippies," or "love it or leave it." Again, such rhetoric demonstrated a lack of multiperspectival thinking. It was disheartening to hear and to read this rhetoric because it did not reflect the new reality of the fractured images.

A day or two after the initial terrorist act on September 11, I joined in a peace vigil held on campus. As candles were lit and people who gathered spoke, we were accosted by jeers from many other college students walking by. One young man in particular yelled and interrupted a speaker, asking how we could say such things. Didn't we care about the innocent people who were killed in New York? And, he assumed, we were calling for peace only because we did not have lost and missing loved ones as he still had. But he was making an erroneous assumption. The decontextualization continued to manifest itself.

As we walked together in the candlelight down the sidewalks of the main street of town to gather at the courthouse, other students opened their apartment windows and blared rock songs at us that they thought were patriotic. They probably did not realize that Bruce Springsteen's "Born in the U.S.A." and Jimi Hendrix's version of the "Star Spangled Banner" were both songs of protest in their historical contexts. But again, the lack of historical contextualization for these young college students who mocked our peace vigil was apparent. Why had no one held up different mirrors for them to see? Our education (or perhaps lack thereof) allows us to remain insulated and decontextualized. Such an insulated worldview, or perhaps better stated, nationview, kept people asking over and over again, "Why would anyone want to do this to us?" But if we are unwilling to look at the multiplicity of refracted reflections, then there is no answer to this question that makes any sense.

During this time, media and public opinion kept the focus pointed outward to an "enemy" outside. Such a focus kept many in denial. Very few chose to deconstruct the superficial patriotism that emerged, and even those who did received little mainstream coverage. In fact, just the opposite occurred: an even stronger dose of superficiality replaced critical judgments previously leveled at our government. For instance, in the recent years and months prior to the 9/11 tragedy, one of the critical and pressing issues was that of police brutality against people of color and racial profiling. Many large metropolitan areas were struggling with this issue and had experienced civil unrest. Although the events of 9/11 have rightly been significant for media coverage, has anyone questioned why we have not returned to the pressing issue of racial profiling and police brutality? We have hailed the bravery of the police officers and firefighters who went into the World Trade Center and perished. This was certainly a terrible loss and we are right to grieve for them. Yet recognizing their bravery, their commitment to their professional work, and the loss experienced by their families does not preclude us from continuing to explore what was going on in police departments prior to 9/11 and what still goes on. Yet we have insulated ourselves and our social institutions once again under another layer of mystification so it will be even more difficult to return to question the injustice existent in racial profiling.

At just the time we need to look into the mirror and crack it the most, we have added layers of mystification to keep our hegemonic social constructions intact. This has occurred in many ways. In my part of the television world, Bill Maher's *Politically Incorrect* show was taken off the air. I guess he said something that was politically incorrect! Rage Against the Machine is an activist political rock band whose lyrics often challenge police and government actions; after 9/11, many radio stations chose not to play their music because their lyrics question power, authority, and social injustice. But their music has always done this. Isn't it important to listen to their music now more than ever for the questions it raises? It appears that many think not. And in our own field, the well-known educational scholar Alfie Kohn (2001, 5) was denied publishing his invited column entitled, "September 11" in *Phi Delta Kappan* when the president of PDK demanded its removal. What was Mr. Kohn's great offense? He asked us to look at our own role in terrorizing and killing in the world at large. He was holding up a mirror that made too many uncomfortable.

The government on both sides of the aisle did not want to enlighten us, educate us, or discuss with us what the lives of many around the world are like on a daily basis. It did not want to do this because it was afraid if we came to some understanding of why the terrorists acted as they did, we might choose not to "go to war" against them. Again, we need an education that will allow us to hold more than one idea at once. Understanding more of why the terrorists did what they did does not mean we have to agree that what they did was justified or correct. We can condemn the act with even more veracity because we have taken the extra step to understand motivation. However one comes down on the issue and the solution, it is a fact that many in the Arab world live with terrorism on a daily basis and the United States plays a role in this. What kind of education will help us understand this dichotomous fact?

Education to Crack the Mirror

In *The Power of Their Ideas,* Deborah Meier (1995) describes her founding work with a group of teachers in a small school in Harlem, New York. At Central Park East and Central Park East Secondary School, a group of teachers worked collaboratively to develop a school that paid attention to the lives of the students and families there. One of the critical components of the curriculum was that it be guided by five habits of mind. Although Meier is careful to let us know that these should not be understood as five hard and fast rules, they have evolved over time and in context to be the building blocks for any particular content. She suggests that their strength is when students are "immersed in their use." They are as follows:

1. Evidence: How do we know what we know?
2. Viewpoint: Who's speaking?
3. Connections and Patterns: What causes what?

4. Supposition: How might things have been different?
5. Why it matters: Who cares? (50)

These five questions make any curriculum relevant, and develop critical thinking as well as problem-based problem-solving cognitive skills that Bloom describes as analysis, synthesis, and evaluation. In an abbreviated way, I would like to imagine how applying these questions to the events of 9/11 might help us understand and consider the event in a more significant, rather than superficial, manner.

How Do We Know What We Know?

Considering this question would certainly have students looking first at the attribution of the terrorist act to Islamic extremists. (Remember the Oklahoma City bombing where the immediate thought turned to Islamic fundamentalists?) It became clear fairly quickly that the actions on 9/11 were associated with Islamic extremists. Even so, before declaring a "war," one would want to know for sure, and there were nations around the world that kept asking for evidence.

As the days and months unfolded, certainly the question of "how do we know what we know?" would pop up again and again as Arabs, Arab-Americans, and Muslims were profiled and stopped, some taken into custody, others taken off of planes, and many denied the civil rights we have come to expect in the United States. This question would have our students questioning the methods and authority of surveillance and intelligence gathering and media reporting. How do we know that this or that Muslim individual should be taken into custody and held? What gives the Federal Bureau of Investigation the power to do that? It would eventually lead to a discussion and understanding of the newly passed "Patriot Act," which has given unprecedented powers to intelligence agencies and the government. But without such an education posing such questions, the "Patriot Act" breezes through Congress and the people of the United States think a good thing has been done. A mirror should have cracked!

Who's Speaking?

This is a fundamental critical question of perspective and multiplicity. Who is speaking when the president of the United States speaks? The people of the United States? When the media speaks? When Osama bin Laden speaks? When people seeking peaceful solutions speak? And are all voices being allowed equal access to the national/international conversation? The follow-up questions would involve whether some voices are heard over others, and why. And what can students do to find the places where alternative voices often have to abide? Gathering knowledge and understanding for analysis and synthesis to take place is a stepping-stone in learning. Asking these hard questions about who has voice and what differential power that voice carries is critical to the health of a democracy.

What Causes What?

This question was asked in certain forms from the moment many U.S. citizens found out about the attack. On my campus I heard many students say, "But why would they want to hurt us?" As students delved into this question, they would find that the superficial answers provided by national leaders were woefully inadequate. The attack did not occur because the terrorists envied American freedom, democracy, or prosperity. Students would have to look outside of the jargon of patriotic response to examine the impact of U.S. foreign policy. By saying this I am by no means implying that anything justified these horrendous acts of terror. But without understanding what leads some people to such extremes, we have little hope of changing the world for the long term and preventing another such tragedy.

When exploring the impact of U.S. foreign policies, students would be asked to deal with the complexity and the historical context of the Middle East, and to gain an understanding of the Abrahamic religions and their historical relations, as well as the contemporary problems that exist in this area of the world and many others, including terrorism in the United States carried out by militia movements, the Aryan Nation, and antiabortion extremists.

How Might Things Have Been Different?

This is a difficult one to entertain because all of us desperately wish that 9/11 were just a dream from which we could awake or a Hollywood movie scene that would be over in ninety minutes. But it cannot be taken back. What, then, is the point of asking how things might have been different? I would hope it helps us see the necessity of looking outward at the impacts of the U.S. presence in the world and of the World Bank policies, and also of looking inward at our own systems of safety. For a number of years prior to 9/11, various investigative news reporters have gathered evidence about how easy it is to breach security at airports, and even former Federal Aviation Administration officials had been on the national news warning us that we must make serious and drastic changes. So why did we not listen? And what might be different if we had? The answers to this question could range anywhere from authorities might have stopped the hijackers before they boarded the planes, to an entire rethinking of U.S. foreign policy.

Who Cares?

The answer to the question "who cares?" seems self-evident in the face of such tragedy. Of course, millions of people cared. The outpouring of concern and sympathy from U.S. citizens and the people and governments from around the world was apparent. But even in a situation that has been so traumatic, it is important to ask this as the days and months go on. While the money poured in for the families of the firefighters and police officers who lost their lives, there were questions raised much more quietly about others who lost their lives who did not carry the same high profile. There were janitors and security personnel and other working-class people who died in the buildings and whose loss left as big a hole in the hearts of their families as that of a firefighter or a high-level executive did. Who cared about them?

Another question that needed to be addressed was about those calling for a peaceful solution rather than a war waged in Afghanistan. As noted earlier, almost every peace vigil or letter to the editor was received as if those calling for peace were not as traumatized and patriotic as those supporting the call to arms from the president. Did they not really care about the tragic loss? Who cares about the citizen Afghans who were killed and continue to be killed? The women and children and other noncombatants in a war that is not really a war? Who cares about the sad irony of our government's calling this a war, but then not allowing the Taliban prisoners to be called "prisoners of war" and accorded protection under the Geneva Convention? Wouldn't we demand that our soldiers and even journalists covering these events be treated justly?

Critical, Questioning, Fragmenting Education

Although one can see this is just the tip of the iceberg, imagine what students would uncover—and the depth of education they would receive—if they applied these five questions to the terror of 9/11. It is critical to understand that how teachers facilitate and guide students through their curriculum, be it in a textbook or from the events of life that cannot be ignored, either opens the world to them or helps hide it. Five simple habits of mind that permeate the curriculum at a small school in Harlem: What a difference it would make if educative habits such as these replaced the current national focus on standards and proficiency testing!

Consider this example described by Michael Apple and James Beane (1995) in *Democratic Schools*. They describe the traditional discussion of current events in a school classroom. At the time it was observed, the class was having a discussion of "natural disasters," and in the news at the time were stories and pictures of the horrendous and massive mudslides taking place in some South American countries. The students obviously felt bad, but Apple and Beane proceed to point out what happens when the lens with which we look at such events is not questioned. When these current events are named "natural disasters," it conveys that there is little anyone can do to prevent them. They are "an act of God," as some might say. But Apple and Beane suggest that there is another important aspect to these events that makes them "natural disasters." Every year, in different parts of the world, it rains and rains, and every year, in different parts of the world, hillsides give way and mudslides happen. What captures our attention and gives the title of "natural disaster" is when human beings are harmed by these events, as they were in this case. The massive mudslides tore through the roughly built shacks on the hillside and injured and killed large numbers of men, women, and children. But the only thing that was natural about this was that torrential rains occurred and the waterlogged hills began to slide. Everything beyond that was created by human beings.

In the situation described by Apple and Beane, it was the case that those who lived on the mountainsides were the poorest of the poor. It was the only land they could afford. No one in the valleys, where the more affluent people lived, was harmed at all. Apple and Beane conclude,

> Poor families are forced to live on the dangerous hillsides because this is the only land left on which they can afford to eke out a meager existence. People crowd onto the mountainsides because of poverty and historical land ownership patterns that are grossly unequal. Hence, the problem is not the yearly rain—a natural occurrence—but the unequal economic structures that allow a small minority of individuals to control the very lives of the majority of people in that region. (14)

Apple and Beane are arguing that we must have education that allows us to see the world in its complexity, its multiplicities. When we do, then we and our students will have a "richer and more ethically committed sensitivity to the societies around them" (14). This is what we wish for ourselves, but it is also what we wish for other societies around the world so that we can prevent tragedies such as the one Apple and Beane describe, and so very importantly, the tragedy of 9/11.

Ultimately, education for the world in which we live must be on a par with the complexity of that world. As such, we must assist our students in becoming comfortable with ambiguity, complexity, and paradox, rather than concrete rights and wrongs, simplicity, and singular worldviews. We must move from education that presents the world as "this *or* that" to an education that can present the world and ourselves as "this *and* that," and not perceive it as a logical contradiction. In the context of Apple and Beane's example, our students need to be able to understand that it *is* a natural disaster and it *is not* a natural disaster, and make complete sense of that. In the tragic example of 9/11, we can assuredly say that it was a senseless, irrational act *and* it is not a senseless, irrational act. Rather than being judged as unpatriotic for such a statement, we need to pursue such thinking in order to come to a fuller understanding of the multiple perspectives present in our world. Such an understanding is one of the most important we can obtain if we hope to prevent such tragedies from occurring on the soil of the United States or of any other nation.

Perhaps a new appreciation can be had of a cracked mirror. Instead of the proverbial bad luck that superstition has implied, we can begin to see that cracking the mirror of the social reflections of our world allows us to see ourselves in the different reflections and refractions of the broken pieces. In so doing, we gain a deeper and more efficacious democratic and critical education that can help us and our students make sense of our world in a way that we hope can diminish the number of tragedies we face. Cracked mirrors provide multiple images simultaneously, and it is through embracing this metaphorical paradox of thinking that these social mirrors may shed new vision for us. If we be willing.

Acknowledgment

I thank Dr. Andi O'Conor for her helpful suggestions on a previous draft of this article and for sharing her own teaching experiences on the day of September 11.

References

Apple, Michael, and James Beane. 1995. *Democratic Schools.* Alexandria, Va.: Association for Supervision and Curriculum Development.
Kohn, Alfie. 2001. "Teaching About September 11th." In *Rethinking Schools: An Urban Education Journal.* Milwaukee, WI: Rethinking Schools, Ltd.
Meier, Deborah. 1995. *The Power of Their Ideas: Lessons for America from a Small School in Harlem.* Boston: Beacon.
Rich, Adrienne. 1989. "Invisibility in Academe." In Renato Rosaldo, *Culture and Truth: The Remaking of Social Analysis.* Boston: Beacon.

Correspondence should be addressed to Jaylynne N. Hutchinson, Ohio University, Department of Educational Studies/McCracken Hall, Athens, OH 45701. E-mail: hutchinj@ohiou.edu

Imagining Ethical Historical Consciousness: Pedagogical Possibilities and the Recent Trauma of September Eleventh

ANDREW N. McKNIGHT
University of North Carolina at Greensboro

The events of September 11 raise important moral, political, and psychological problems concerning the state and future of the human race. They also raise considerable pedagogical questions concerning how issues of social justice and historical trauma can and should be approached in educational spaces. In this article, I first explore my own pedagogical reactions to the tragedies in New York and Washington, D.C., and the Middle East. The discussion contin-

ues with a theoretical examination of the numerous emotional issues surrounding the pedagogical address of trauma, and the formation of reparative
strategies concerning how we exist in the world. At the heart of this piece is the
conviction that these concerns must be addressed in pedagogical spaces if we
are to seek a more humane human community, and if we are to reach more
beneficial emotional states of existence.

I sat in front of my eleven o'clock undergraduate foundations class with the intention to teach *something*, a decision that, in fact, I am still questioning from both
a practical and an ethical standpoint. I am now confronted with questions concerning my readiness, or even competence, to broach the topic. The brief space between class and my witness of the images and narratives surrounding that morning's events casts serious doubt regarding how completely I had grasped what had
happened.

I confess to intellectualizing almost immediately after hearing the
events—groping for the historical-political causes, moral implications, and possible future recourse. Perhaps, as a defense mechanism, I wished to assuage emotion
in favor of a retreat into mind, into sublimated causes, effects, and solutions. However, forcing this type of inquiry on my students out of my own inability to emotionally assimilate my experience of the tragedy, may have been premature. Perhaps my determination to teach, rather than just cancel class, was spurred by a
misplaced sense of the Protestant work ethic, a compulsion to teach for its own
sake, or for an institutional commitment. Or, perhaps, I felt some nagging moral
obligation to make this an "educative moment," to address what I had been hitherto
intellectualizing regarding possible causes. But maybe I just wanted some people
to talk to for a while. After all, not an hour earlier, as I was getting ready to walk to
campus, a friend called and hastily and disquietedly told me to turn on my television because "a plane has hit the World Trade Center."

So, there I sat with my class, in detached disbelief, groping for rational answers
and intending to teach. I must confess, as alluded to previously, that part of my interest in teaching was probably selfish: I myself wanted to process the images and texts
that just an hour before I had watched, via mass media, unfold. The assigned readings
for the day discussed obedience and authority in school, but although related in some
ways, and inextricable in others, to the social impetus and catalyst responsible for the
actions taken by the terrorists, I felt they were largely unsubstantial and ineffectual in
the face of this particular situation. The abruptness and strangeness of the morning's
events required a different approach, not a formal lesson or stylized discussion, but
an embodied conversation. Through my own emotional disarray, I asked my students what they had heard and where. And we spent the first fifteen minutes asking
questions of one another concerning the facts of the situation, so far as we were able
to discern them at that point. Most of the questions regarded the what, where, when,
and hows of the situation. While this was proceeding, and then obviously fading, I

hastily came up with two questions for discussion: Why did this happen? and What circumstances create this kind of human behavior?

The students were responsive. Some surprised me with their knowledge of Mideast politics and the United States's policies concerning the region. Although the discussion was somber, it never became expressively emotional. Some of the students admitted sadness and fear, but I feel that the events were of such immediate proximity that most of what we were able to discern was starkly factual. They spoke of the dynamics of control versus autonomy and freedom; the difference between alienation and membership; between helplessness and confusion and meaning and purpose. In some ways, the assigned readings for the day seeped into the discussion and gave it play and context. The class cognitively named and understood the conditions that could have led to feelings of oppression on the part of poor or socially disenfranchised people. They also understood how this could be exploited by the megalomaniacal.

However, in my effort to seek intellectual resolution, I ignored possibly the most appropriate response at that point, which was to feel, emote, and share these experiences with one another. We needed solidarity and accompanying feelings of understanding and security. We needed to grieve the lives of the victims, at least to some extent, and lament the circumstances that created this breech of human dignity, love, and responsibility. It may have been too soon for that, or that I was subconsciously unwilling, or emotionally unable, to create such a pedagogical space. My questions concerning the whys and hows, although intended to elicit emotional *and* intellectual responses, explicitly favored the latter. By assigning the necessity of cause, I precluded from the discourse personal reaction concerning its nascent obfuscating ambiguity and emotional absurdity. Its rawness was replaced by a mad dash toward rationalization and the possibility of reparative strategies, both important but inappropriate considering the proximity of the event. My control occluded much from the discursive landscape (time, connection of experiences, etc.). My questions were pointed and purposeful, but pointed nonetheless, and therefore prescriptive in connotation.

Since then, the question that has preyed upon my conscience as an educator concerns the construction of pedagogical encounters that would at once be relational, emotionally healing, *and* that could possibly yield reparative strategies in the form of present social and political action. What should be the initial pedagogical response and how should it proceed if it wishes to achieve, at the student's discretion, the aforementioned categories?

In this article I will examine the construction of pedagogical encounters that memorialize, emotionally validate, critique, and reflect upon traumatic events like those of September 11. The following will provide a cursory examination of what denotes an ethical affective-pedagogical encounter, the role of educator in facilitating this encounter, and what socioethical obligations this engenders. This involves fleshing out and concretizing critical-theoretical orientations in the light of the current situation in conjunction with ideas of affective practice. The intention is to form a praxis of social philosophy and critical pedagogy that looks at historical issues and the potential for transformative emotional reaction and critical historical inquiry through discourse and experiential encounters with texts, as semiotic, tactile, or visual representations. Examples might include written narratives of description or opinion concerning a past context; enduring and extant objects from the past, natural or manufactured; or images both static and as real-time footage of an event as it transpired.

The pedagogical problems surrounding past travesties against humanity, the remembrance of historical trauma, and encounters with difficult knowledge like the events of September 11, are discussed in the next section. Following this is a brief analysis of how traumatic events like September 11 generate a plethora of texts, and how our consciousness references symbols based on experience of interpersonal-dialogical, and physical-natural, dialectics.

Confronting difficult knowledge, historical trauma, and the legacies these manifest in the present are complicated in their social context and are delicate spaces for pedagogical application. This critical-pedagogical nexus of emotional responses and information (historical records, narratives, testimonies, etc.) is a site of potentially uneasy confrontations. However, it is a space where individuals may come together with the possibility of forming a community of learners for the sake of interpersonal understanding and political effect. The salient yet formidable and perplexing question remains to determine what an appropriate pedagogical response to trauma should involve. What shall be experienced, what shall be discussed, when attempted, by whom, with what obligations and expectations on the part of all participants, and for what potential moral social-use value? These issues will be addressed in the body of the article, with specific attention paid to the September 11 tragedy.

Finally, I will conclude with a brief argument for the ethicality and practicality of the pedagogies discussed toward the benefit of our shared humanity. Key to this thesis are the psychological and rational considerations that may contribute to healthy physical, emotional, and intellectual living conditions.

The Pedagogical Problem of September 11th

Intellectually, the ramifications and intricacies of this present imbroglio are multifarious and emotionally difficult to apprehend. It is also a profound site of anger and grief for the citizens of the United States and for many in other nations who share our sorrow and indignation. The problems it raises concerning the state of the world are sociopolitical, but they are also pedagogical. Somehow, we must learn to emotionally cope with the current circumstances and sate our critical and emotional wills to provide much needed meaning concerning the causes and consequences of the events. This pedagogy needs to circumvent debilitating guilt, helplessness, denial, or resentment if we retain any hope of emotional reconciliation and appropriate critical-ethical action. It must do so for the sole purpose of confronting emotional confusion in its nascency in dialogical space to create individual and public understanding, rather than private reified withdrawal into the previously mentioned categories.

We should also ascertain what knowledge and what ethical orientations shall inform our reparative actions in the present toward the future. Our methods of healing, and reparative proposals, require addressing both the anguish engendered by an event we cannot change, and the anxiety and uncertainty over the implications it holds for the future of humankind. Through this uncertainty, individuals in pedagogical solidarity should begin to address the horrific manner and context in which these events were carried out; begin to own and explore their emotions; and also begin to consider critically, cause, result, and appropriate ethical actions.

In general terms outside of the specific nature of the recent tragedies, the task for socially conscious educators is to set in motion pedagogical projects that have the potential to attend to past traumas, both immediate and distant, extant in our social memories and ontic material circumstances. It should be stated candidly that pedagogies of this type will not inevitably "fix" these problems by their application via grand amelioration; nor will the memories of past trauma, or the witness of past trauma through textual encounters, necessitate a transcendence of memories and experience toward their irrelevance and disappearance. There is no final eschatological outcome. Examination of these issues is nothing short of an examination of our daily existences, and the negotiation of our circumstances.

Memories and textual experiences must be constantly held in a state of contextual and interpretative flux; they must find themselves in constant critical application and reach a conscious state of affective knowledge that allows for cross-referencing across similar situations. Although certainly not a societal panacea, each new connection, each understanding of cause, each textual link to the stuff of our existence renders our ability to name our experience and circumstance more acute. Our world thus becomes larger, more complex, yet it also become more ours, more intimate, and more receptive to intersubjective freedom and reciprocity through a recognition of common circumstances.

Texts and Symbols

Texts generally generate references to cultural symbols that signify our embedded social memories. The individual conceptual variations concerning the meanings and import of such symbols, and what multifarious meanings and questions they engender concerning their connection to our world-stage, are as numerous as individual consciousnesses. However, the symbols themselves assume a more general significance for the culture as a whole, for they serve as emotional communicative centers of individual textual interpretation. For Dewey ([1929]1958), these

centers "are condensed substitutes of actual things and events, which embody actual things with more direct and enhanced import" (83).

Humans, from memory and ritual, conjure symbols from texts that come into
our lines of perception, like the images of the Trade Center victims and their loved
ones, the physical destruction of the buildings, the president's call for swift justice,
and the mysterious and frightening pictures of possible Arab perpetrators, to name
but a few. Symbols generally dormant in the cynical and alienated social landscape
of the United States, like the flag, have once again become "centre[s] of emotionally charged behavior" (82). It is in these symbols that we find commonality. The
risk, however, is that these symbols can also become sites of manipulation by the
powerful or of false and jingoistic hubris. The idealized outcomes spoken of later
in this article by Deborah Britzman could also include adherence to an unethical
form of xenophobic and dogmatic patriotism that substitutes mob membership for
moral responsibility.

Critically, we must be able to view these symbols not as reified, but something
to name, examine, and pragmatically determine ethical social use-value. This involves naming the underlying emotions behind these socially created and located
symbols, and their causes. As Dewey states, these symbols are active manifestations of our emotional selves: "the feature which characterizes symbolism is pre-
cisely that the thing which later reflection calls a symbol is not a symbol, but a direct vehicle, a concrete embodiment, a vital incarnation" (82). These infinite
permutations of relationship, our intersubjective reflection and naming, envelops
the human condition. Examination of immediate texts may serve as a cathartic catalyst for self-reflection and embodied communal action through examinations of
social relationships as interpretative ontological exercises. The exercises represent
a way in which we use inquiry to provide cultural analysis of symbol-generating
phenomena, and also affirm aspects of our existence through an affirmation of
commonality.

The witnessed phenomena in this particular case, September 11, are painfully
obvious and explicitly potent. The pedagogical examination of dominant referent
symbols invoked by this instance may serve as a vehicle for critical reflection and
embodied communal action. These symbols are not unilaterally deleterious to re-
ciprocal human harmony, nor do they necessarily contradict positive social sentiments. They may even be sites of solidarity and the affirmation of moral community; regardless, we need to be cognizant of their impetus and potentials, both as
beneficial and detrimental to ethical freedom.

There is an obvious and profound need for discourse about the symbols of freedom and oppression alike. For instance, pedagogical attempts could be deployed to
discursify and determine what constitutes healthy and ethical patriotism and what
our moral obligations are concerning other human cultures and nations in the
global community. These themes are addressed throughout the remainder of the article, so for now I shall move on.

The next section, and the body of the article, addresses the way in which texts can be utilized in a pedagogy that emphasizes emotional response to trauma. Critical inquiry concerning the nature of these emotions, and of the symbols engendered by our memories and experiences, is also examined in an attempt to expand our communal expressions of critical historical consciousness and ethical action.

Trauma and Remembrance

Roger Simon, Sharon Rosenberg, and Claudia Eppert (1999) state in the introduction to *Between Hope and Despair: Pedagogy and the Remembrance of Historical Trauma* that remembrance and pedagogy are "an indissoluble couplet.... [necessary for the] formation and regulation of meanings, feelings, perceptions, identifications, and the imaginative projection of human limits and possibilities" (2). The pedagogical project of historical remembrance brings to bear issues of particular contemporary importance, things from the past that still live in our present, "an 'unworked-through past,' a past that continues to pose questions" (4).

In the specific case of September 11, our past is viscerally present and profoundly unworked-through. The stages of our individual cognition concerning these events are divergent and diffuse. Memories of what has been witnessed, and of our reactions and connections, reference experience immediate and distant. These disparate cognitive locations are an uncertain and uneven terrain from which to begin critical pedagogical application, and to engage in the critical inquiry of texts. Memories are often sites of guilt, shame, and confusion for the oppressors and oppressed alike, and in this context, it may be the case that we are both. It is also difficult to discern where emotional relations emanate from, and if these spaces are even directly related to the events at hand. Regardless of where the emotion finds its genesis, an affective pedagogy must begin by addressing the projection itself, the deed or unrequited emotional response, and then make determinations concerning its relevance. Once potential relevance has been established, potentially unpleasant emotional and memorial connections to troubling past narratives and images may provide a vital outlet for conducting accurate encounters with present emotional wounding, and its connection to unethical aspects of societal life.

Central to this is the need for communal pedagogy. The project of historical remembrance compels us to "view historical consciousness as always requiring another, as an indelibly social praxis, a very determinate set of commitments and actions held and enacted by members of collectivities" (Simon et al. 1999, 2). These collectivities are evident for they envelop and shape the stuff of our entire lived social experience. It is not enough to supply formative influences for an isolated moral consciousness; one must act morally in accordance with the consciousness and existence of others. To paraphrase Sartre, we experience our freedom through interactions for and with, and in reference to, others.[1] Thus, to work through a traumatic experience like September 11 requires a community of free knowing subjects, a plurality of learners willing to share reactions and interpretations and provide emotional support if need be.

In pragmatic tenor, the authors state, "remembrance as a strategic response posits a continuity between the living and the dead by collapsing the latter's specificities into our contemporary political and social use-value" (Simon et al. 1999, 5). The political potentials and pedagogical problems posed by attempting to reconcile historical trauma toward hope of a more just future are numerous. To begin, it is an unsettling pedagogy that forces students to remember or come to understand the remembrance of others, and engage in an emotionally laden historical exegesis, in this case concerning immediate events possibly suppressed and repressed in their specificities.

The pedagogical-historical nexus of "present consciousness and the staging of evidentiary traces of past presence" (Simon et al. 1999, 10) involves using personal memorial insight as a source for interaction with testimony that illuminates the experience referent or analogous to the memory. Simon states that the memory's author may elicit empathy in comparison to an event through "a point of connection … similar to elements of one's experience" (12). This affective connection does not necessarily denote prior participation in the event's inception and execution, but it does require that the event be *witnessed*, in some sense, by the student.

Texts, both fictional and nonfictional (historically located texts and objects) may yield critical and affective pedagogical encounters. They may serve as the vehicle for pertinent examinations that synthesized, and objectively analyzed, macro accounts, for example, social statistics, may be unable to provide. With primary source texts like narratives and images, there is the potential for an immediacy of interpretation and of emotional connection to the biographical significance of the author's deeds, possible explanation of the intentions and environmental factors leading to the outcomes, and possible revelations regarding the quality and character of the actor's life. In the case of September 11, the texts include those of cause, for example, Islamic fundamentalism, U.S. foreign policy, the political history of the region, and the various written and oral reactions of people around the globe concerning the situation at hand. The authors range from historians, political figures, and clerics to journalists and photographers. The actors include all cognizant of the tragedy, from students in the United States to starving Afghans.

The art of witnessing finds its nascency in being "open to the possibility of an unforseen memory" (Simon et al. 1999, 19) of what the participant was not involved in but is implicated in by virtue of his or her awareness of it, and its impending presence in current social conditions. This "remembrance initiates forms of learning that shift and disrupt the present, opening one to new ways of perceiving, thinking, and acting" (13) through a heightened awareness of past experience and of our own places and potentials within the societal order. In some ways this may be difficult in the current instance. The distance between analysis and event is close, and the range of emotional responses broad and mercurial. The possibility of affect lies in our mass witness of the events of September 11, regardless if we have an immediate cognitive-experiential point of reference.

The Fall

Succinctly put, affective educational encounters with past traumas begin either with remembrance or witness, and reach their emotional import in a "fall" (27), to be discussed shortly; and hopefully, through subsequent critical inquiry, find some reconciliation and committed impetus to formulate and commit ethical acts toward amelioration and solidarity. The initial reaction or *fall,* for our purposes here, represents shock, denial, anger, revelation, discomfort, despair, and so on, that one may experience during an encounter with traumatic past texts or memories. It denotes the denudation of our coping strategies, denials and sublimations, leaving the encounter intimate and the individual vulnerable, doubting, and critical. When a student experiences a *fall* it is generally through a brutal revelation of recalled memory or witness that leaves her personally unsure, yet deeply implicated in the world. Through this uncertainty, she must begin not only to question her most deep-seeded interpretations of the world, but her place within it. Like Clamence in Albert Camus's ([1957]1991) *The Fall* trying to fathom his entanglement in the world that allowed 6 million Jews to be murdered. His crimes enveloped those of the world, and he came to the stark realization of universal responsibility. His *fall* ends with the conclusion that "every man [sic] testifies to the crime of all the others—that is my faith and my hope" (110).

The *fall* into a feeling of ultimate responsibility provides the psychological seed-ground for the reconciliation of failures to act ethically, wounds suffered, and responsibility in the face of witness and encounter with memories, texts and experiences not examined, repressed, or sublimated. It implicates the participants irrevocably as responsible members of a shared humanity.

What induces a *fall* may include an examination of memory, both as transmitted aspects of inherited oral traditions, dispositions, and epistemological lenses, and as experiences both lived and as witnessed encounters with texts. It represents the moment when false memory, or just general ignorance, is exposed, leaving the critical rational mind emotionally raw to attempt to make sense of the information, to reconcile conflicting emotions, to create knowledge, and to formulate possible implications for action in the present.

For instance, we can no longer hold the naive belief that the United States is a safe, detached, and innocent oasis apart from a violent world. The moral upheaval that saturates and plagues our recent memories invokes a need for criticality that can be denied no longer. Our materially privileged and emotionally detached perch from which we have been able to view the rest of the world and its travesties has, in many ways, been destroyed along with our citizens' lives and symbolic architecture. Thus, we must face our implications concerning the larger whole, and our complacency concerning violence, not just in our immediate environment, but also in areas previously thought to be irrelevant to our daily lives. It requires that we rescue ourselves from what Maxine Greene (1988) refers to as the sunken everydayness of life and the macrobanality that masks the personal immediacy of trauma and tragedy wrought by the terrorist acts.

Out of this critical awakening we begin to engage in an *action dialectic* between emotional response and critical analysis/reason: the constant interplay between our emotions and our rational minds. The former provides the stimulus and passion for the latter's analysis and its decision-making capabilities. The challenge is to determine how students can move from emotional responses, that is, the *fall,* to critical analysis and eventually to the emotional desire to unpack the social meaning of texts, assume appropriate responsibility, and propagate more universal expressions of human freedom through their actions.

The *fall* in this instance, regardless of the nature of its affect, first emerges with the critical engagement—witness—of the events of, and circumstances surrounding, September 11. This means coming to grips with the image of the plane hitting the buildings, and of the buildings' collapse, replayed ad infinitum via mass media. The texts generated in this immediate case concerned the physical specifics of the violence, the presumed dead and injured, the United States's instant resolve to seek retribution, and images and testimony of the grieving.

With each image and narrative the world became larger, more confusing, and more uncertain, and more potentially dangerous. Obviously the risk for educators is that without proper attention, students may slip into denial of events; paralyzing fear of death; displacement of anger upon the less powerful, for example, Arab- and Muslim Americans; or despair without hope of reparations. All of this comes at the risk of uncritically ignoring our emotional lives and reinforcing and perpetuating dominant and routinized hegemonic power structures that may have contributed to these events in the first place.

The Problems of Pedagogical Outcomes

Coping with the realities of the situation as we perceive and conceive of, and are affected by, them is contingent largely on who we are—our experiential location and psychological state—and what emotional proximity we held in relation to the actual events of September 11. One pedagogical obligation, however unpleasant, is to encounter and affirm the texts, both visual and semantic, as potentially eliciting emotions such as grief, anger, empathy and sympathy, repression, sublimation, displacement, melancholia, anguish, fear, resentment, projection, isolation, and intellectualization, to name but a few psychological categories.

Deborah Britzman (in Simon et al. 1999), however, warns about what she considers to be common mistakes made in the engagement of historical texts. She believes that too often engagements with texts (her example is the diary of Anne

Frank) encourage "idealized outcomes of learning; perhaps the most common concerns the inscription of hope" (28). It may be the case that, in our mad rush to the comforting shores of hope, we miss the real affective and critical encounter; we may miss the moments of discomfort that would lead to different states of consciousness and thus different loci of ethical action. She states, "idealization may be one way to avoid the painful dilemmas of confronting the traumatic residues of this [the Holocaust] devastating history" (29). Once again, we confront the problems of reluctance and avoidance that Simon spoke of earlier. Not only is it our tendency frequently to soften the impact of such narratives, but we also wish to avoid even the potential for such discomfort.[2]

Another pedagogical problem arises when specific didactic outcomes are expected or required of a learning experience. We cannot artificially expect emotional responses; we cannot expect everyone to grieve, nor can we expect students not to exhibit emotions other than the ones we might intend or wish for. However, we can at least provide conditions where this type of connection might be possible, if not encouraged. Concerning the present lack of pedagogical engagement of historical texts, Britzman (in Simon et al. 1999) posits,

> Thought that invokes action responds to what went before, and being forced
> back into thought after our actions allows for a revision of the time of experi-
> ence, opening experience to something more than the immediacy of our needs,
> our capacity to disavow the ramification of traumatic events, and the obscurity
> of recognizing historical breakdowns in our own times. (30)

A pedagogy that revisits these experiences can potentially assist in the analysis of our raw perception concerning the events of September 11, encourage critical thought and personal reflection, and promote ethical reparative strategies.

Critical inquiry of an affective nature is sine qua non to the pedagogical process of historical analysis for ethical action based in changes in historical consciousness. It allows for uncomfortable thoughts to be held and analyzed without the risk of succumbing to easy unreflective complacency. The need for affective critical inquiry into the past is tacit, especially when the emotional content of that history is consciously palpable or materially tangible. Emotion and experience are inseparable to any pedagogical encounter, and exceptionally relevant when confronting historical trauma.

One prime educative moment in critical historical inquiry is the point of vulnerability when feelings of personal loss can assume aspects of another's loss. The project is to embrace the trauma and to work past our discomfort with and for others. It is as Britzman (Simon et al. 1999) states, "to make an ethical relation to the stranger, to encounter vulnerability as a relation and thus move beyond the impulse of repeating the trauma by placing helplessness and loss elsewhere" (35). In this, teachers must be willing to personally relate their own encounters with traumatic witness with the students in a critical and emotionally attuned community of learning; they need to be aware of their own pain and confusion and be receptive to the pain and confusion of others.

The goals of this type of pedagogy, emotional reconciliation and ethical action, have already been emphasized. Jacques Derrida, quoted in Britzman's (Simon et al. 1999) essay, echoes this aspiration: "to learn to live *with* ghosts, in the upkeep, the conversation, the company, or the companionship, in the commerce without commerce of ghosts. To live otherwise, and better. No, not better, but more justly. But *with them*" (40). We need to work through aggression, complacency, shame, and guilt concerning things that were not of our direct cause, but may be of our perpetuation. We need to determine ways, in community, of working through the trauma of oppressed, and often dead, others so as not to transfer this malevolence to future others and thus perpetuate these hegemonic injustices. We also need to recognize that history exists in a dialectic between action and memory that is continuously unfolding. As Britzman urges, our pedagogical projects must accept history as an "unfinished story" (50), and thus not determined. It must be actively sought and lived.

Pedagogies of trauma and critical historical inquiry also need to avoid sentimentalization that shuns transformation in favor of easy emotional catharsis and hasty conciliation. It also needs to avoid romanticizing historical actors implicated in a traumatic event as mere objects of projection and idealized fantasy and thus unreal and detached from present lived circumstances and suffering therein. Critical pedagogues need to address the lives of present actors and present social problems when we inquire about the past, and avoid anemic and innocuous or contrived and formulaic discussions of "current events." Didactic equivalents of quick-fix pop-therapy nostrums may lead to events of real import being responded to with emotional banality. Nor can shoddy realpolitik solutions, those that correspond to vulgar utilitarian ends, be any substitute for sustained and pointed ethical-political deliberations.

We need to try, to grieve, to learn to live with the emotional weight of these events. But, we also need to ask questions and enlist the help of our intellects toward personal and social healing and reparative political actions. The questions raised are unavoidably problematic, and raise even more recondite implications for our negotiation of the vagaries of the human condition. To examine something from the position of necessary emotional connection requires a willingness to keep both emotion and powers of rational ordering, verification, and use in active interpretive space. The field of interpretation is therefore mercurial and needs to be pedagogically negotiated as such.

A first step in the process toward critical historical consciousness is to break cycles of complacency and ignorance. Much oppression is experienced through resignation reified by the shear mundaneness of routine repetition. People become conditioned by the mechanical nature of their daily lives, their alienation from their social and physical production, and their role as labor commodity in the larger social scheme. As Marcuse (1973) states, "this link is fastened in the individuals themselves; the needs of a repressive society have become their own; social compulsion appears as the liberty of the individual" (221). The oppression is internalized falsely as liberty in the sense that it is a universal condition, and that there is some security to be found in conformity. "The liberty of the master goes hand in hand with the liberty of the slave" (220), once the latter accepts, consciously or subconsciously, the systemic precepts of oppression.

However, in time of crisis, these usually sublimated or repressed problems often come to the fore. In the case of September 11, the internal schism between what many feel concerning swift and brutal retaliation, and the desire for the United States to do the morally correct thing, speaks volumes. In a time of patriotism unprecedented in recent memory, many are also aware of the poverty experienced in many Mideast nations, the violence toward women, the oppression of the majority by the wealthy, and the deleterious effects that much of U.S. foreign policy has had on the region. Most want to be good people, to act responsibly, and to not cause unnecessary suffering, but we are also perplexed and apprehensive about our own place and safety in the world.

The "point of connection," as a way to break these sublimated hegemonic cycles spoken of by Simon (1999), is contingent upon the ability to assimilate others' memories "within the memorial boundaries that circumscribe one's identity identifications" (12), and is problematized somewhat by the memory of an unknowable other, of circumstances that cannot become tenable. In her essay *Responding to the Ethical Address of Past and Present Others,* Claudia Eppert (in Simon et al. 1999) traces the difficulty in creating personal understanding of others' experience:

> I was struck with the singular awareness that my questions of a text, of others, could never be fully realized in an answer. Insofar as my questions constituted the pursuit of a particular conclusive truth, they would always be insufficient and require more questions. I learned that the subject to which my questions were directed would never be reducible to them, that *I would never know.* In this context, I began to wonder what it means to question, what and how one learns from questioning, and how the orientation of questioning enables or obstructs responsible engagement with others. (214)

Who were, and who are, the victims, and what are our responsibilities to them? The lives of the people inside those airplanes and buildings; the fear, panic, and suffering they endured; and the suffering and grief that still lingers in the holes left in the lives of friends, relatives, and witnesses, primary and otherwise, casts a wide net of those in need. Remembrance of this trauma may need to be unresolved and kept suspended in interpretive flux, for it to be reconciled in its tragic and ambiguous nature, somewhere between peaceful harmony and chaotic discord.

Our responsibility is to address the various responses of all of those affected, even when those responses may be initially detrimental to the individual, or immoral to the world. For instance, the vengeful desire of some to "turn Afghanistan into a parking lot," cannot be merely dismissed as morally repugnant if we wish to have ethical action as a result of our pedagogies. Although this view does ignore the historical reality that Afghanistan already is, regrettably for the people who reside there and attempt sustenance on that land, a parking lot. Most of its infrastructure has been decimated by twenty years of invading armies and resulting internal martial strife among the various religious and ethnic cabals. Although the aforementioned desire for vengeance does not speak to justice or love, or a desirable mode of life potentially free, or at least less vulnerable, from future acts of mass violence, it does speak to a very real place in many of our emotional repositories. In present form it represents a potentially deleterious scratching of an affectively embedded, yet uncritically resolved, itch. How does this anger get transformed into ethically appropriate, beneficial, and reparative aims, and what texts and memories need to be encountered and examined?

Pedagogies of Responsibility

Needed is an affirmation of the uniqueness of individual life while holding in critical abeyance the grief surrounding the event as a tragic aberration to the whole of humanity. A dialectical cycle is required that vacillates between the particular, that is, the individual, and his or her inherent and unalienable worth, and the human whole. This also precludes the possibility of an other—an individual or group that we view as being outside of humanity, and thus less than human.

However, what is pedagogically uncomfortable is the distinct possibility that empathy, the ability to assume an authentic understanding of another's trauma, is impossible. We may also fear that the options this leaves us with concerning potential future action may only emanate from learned affectation rather than connected affect. Finding equivalence between a traumatic event and an individual student's experience may prove to be difficult. The notion that all historical situations can be reexperienced in some semblance of their original emotional manifestation is dubious. Where, then, do we draw hope of connection and empathetic interpretation? The dialectical-pedagogical aporia rests in the inability to find common purpose, rather than equivalence in experience. Even if an event is radically foreign in cultural context or in geography, it may find a sort of equivalence in terms of a shared humanity. This also begs the pragmatic question that, even if connectedness is the result of an affectation rather than an authentic cognizance of others' lived experience, could it still lead to more moral social interactions via a mythos of shared existence?

The solution, in so far as there is one, seems to compel us to assume a universal responsibility for the suffering of others. Emmanuel Levinas, as examined by Eppert (in Simon et al. 1999), believes there exists "an a priori structure of relationality and obligation for others ... an infinite and absolute responsibility for that person" (222). The very presence of another and their existential circumstance creates an absolute dialectic of responsibility, a "'difficult freedom,' in which we find ourselves free only to the extent that we are indefinitely and absolutely responsible for others before ourselves" (222).

This implies we should support and engage in pedagogies that don't necessarily locate their impetus solely in empathy, but responsibility, even for those things we may not be able to grasp or to hold as part of ourselves in rational or emotional explanation. In this we recognize that we are these individuals who died; we embody their loss almost as if it were our own, or that of those within our immediate associations. We are the group, those who mourn and grieve the whole of humanity's loss. We are also the terrorists, in that we carry the same human potential for evil as well as good.

Learning is not then a purely self-driven existential affair but is bound up in the presence of the other's narrative and circumstance. It is not simply the attempt to understand the experiences of others but to actualize a certain responsibility engendered by engagement with the other—"from one's encounters with the alterity of a unique other" (Simon et al. 1999, 222). And although "the alterity of another remains irreducible to the learning subject, incapable of being masterfully 'known'" (222), it assumes the burden of responsibility for that which is not, or cannot be, known. Eppert states, "Learning is not the recollection of something already known, but more fundamentally the learning of something new ... [;]it is the experience of something radically foreign" (222).

For instance, we cannot, under absolute alterity, pedagogically seek a perceived equivalency between, say, the violence visited upon Irish, Italian, or Polish immigrants, and the Holocaust, or the trauma of the middle passage/American slavery. Of the latter two examples, the former is still alive in the memories of first- and second-generation witnesses, with present-day manifestations in contemporary anti-Semitism; the latter exists in a more distant mnemonic context but is still very much present in the contours of our social fabric and in the lived experiences of ancestors of the enslaved. However, both engender a responsibility of remembrance and of acting for the past, but also for acting ethically within the present cultural hegemony. The first examples, although still part of our cultural memory, lack immediate connection to the social ills of the present. But, they still may provide useful insight into the dynamics of xenophobia as it may exist in the present. All examples, however, require us to examine our responsibility.

Similarly, the suffering of the families and friends of the victims of the recent attack, and of the nation, are of much different immediacy and emotional import. Not less tragic is the poverty endured by the people of Afghanistan and the violence and repression visited upon the women of that country. However, these are certainly not equivalent in context or affect. Which is worse? That would depend on who you asked. Does it matter? For the purposes of universal expressions of responsibility for the dignity of all humans, the answer is no. The injustice of these events, and the lives of those who live in Afghanistan, lies in the horrible nature of the individual losses and oppression, respectively, and in the ripples this generates across our shared existence.

It is not as simple as exposing students to aspects of other cultures with the intention of raising awareness, dispelling stereotypes, affirming diversity, and encouraging tolerance. Although the aforementioned goals are necessary components of social education, we must be willing to take the additional step toward Martin Buber's (1996) realization that "relation is reciprocity ... inscrutably involved, we live in the currents of universal reciprocity" (67). Affirmation of cultural differences should stress our salient common humanity and universal responsibility for ethical relationship.

The legacy of the historical past and the immediacy of responsibility of first- and second-generation witnesses is supported by Kurt Vonnegut (1969) in his novel *Slaughterhouse Five:* "When a person dies he [sic] only appears to die. He [sic] is still very much alive in the past, so it is very silly for people to cry at his [sic] funeral. All moments, past, present, and future, always have existed, always will exist" (26). Our past often leaves wounds that can be altered in critical ways toward veracity and reconciliation, or toward exacerbation. The difficulty of truth and healing is echoed by one of Vonnegut's characters, who was institutionalized after accidentally shooting a teenage fireman he mistook for a German soldier at the close of World War II. Voicing feelings of both trauma and meaninglessness, he stated to an attending psychiatrist, "You guys are going to have to come up with a lot of wonderful *new* lies, or people just aren't going to want to go on living" (101). The lack of connection and relevancy, of spiritual purpose, that calls into question the justness of this act of violence, even in the context of the Nazi defeat, is dangerous to purposeful remembrance. The just response is, of course, not to create lies as salves for past oppression, but to accept responsibility for our actions and for tragedies endured by others in concert with, and if possible for, their present well-being.

The creation of lies as a psychoanalytic tool has the effect of placing the wounded as an object to be manipulated by healers without any mention of genuine cause. To seek healing without collectively attempting to change social circumstances is tantamount to denial of actual historical experience. Bearing witness to the tragedies of September 11 without profoundly desiring to live in a more just and loving world is paradoxical. It causes the perpetuation of the very conditions, attitudes, and modes of living that fomented the iniquities in the first place. Thus, pedagogically, the questions we pose as students of narratives are "an indeterminably responsive/responsible" (Simon et al. 1999, 226) act, one in which the primacy of self itself becomes questioned and compromised by the presence of another's situation. It necessitates a "self-interrogation [that] might involve asking questions of the personal, social, and historical origins" (227) of the stories behind our reflexive encounter with radically unfamiliar stories.

Ultimately, this change from self/other individualistic protection to one of commonality requires acknowledgment and forgiveness for lack of responsibility in the past. It is important here to distinguish between guilt and responsibility. Guilt entails a kind of responsibility for the perpetration of, or conspiring to participate in, a given act. Guilt in some ways is an easier proposition—if one is guilty, an authority of some sort (obviously some are preferable to others) may punish or seek reparations from the offender. A guilty person—one that is guilty of a specific ethical transgression with genuine consequences—may also provide the latter of his or her own accord, as pertinent to their conscience or other innate, or socially produced, psychological states that may lead to guilty feelings.

If we imagine a less determined and closed moral universe where guilt is a not simply a relative position depending on one's location in the social hierarchy, a universal expression of responsibility can take into account extant power structures as something given but not ultimate or permanent. It affirms a potential leveling up of human capacities and desires toward higher states of creativity, criticality, and expression, and greater levels of moral reciprocity. Responsibility, writ large, is the universal human condition that determines the freedom of others as being directly correlated and coterminous with the freedom that we possess. Others' oppression creates the potential for our own unfreedom in kind.

Hannah Arendt (Smith 1971), in her analysis of the Nazis and the question of German culpability, came to the conclusion that certainly many Germans were explicitly guilty of crimes against humanity, but the scope of responsibility extended well past the Nazi territories. Her conclusion is perhaps an uncomfortable thought for many in our atomistic and hyper-individualistic liberal democracies. She states,

> For the idea of humanity, when purged of all sentimentality, has the very serious consequence that in one form or another men [sic] must assume responsibility for all crimes committed by men [sic] and that all nations share the onus of evil committed by all others. Shame at being a human being is the purely individual and still non-political expression of this insight. (267)

The sociopolitical requirement for critical remembrance is that the public and private must become blurred, if not eliminated, for us to see our experiences and inquiries as bound up in the communal act of assuming responsibility for the experiences and inquiries of others. Students must realize that it matters not that six thousand died in the Trade Center towers and on the airplanes that destroyed them, for this detracts from the fact that all unnecessary human loss and suffering is tragic, lamentable, and should be cause for reflection, grief, critical inquiry, and ethical reparative action.

Concluding Remarks

Actualizing the "human limits and possibilities" of remembrance spoken of earlier requires "*strategic practice* in which memorial pedagogies are deployed for their sociopolitical value and promise. ... a *difficult return,* a psychic and social responsibility to bring the dead into presence, a responsibility that concurrently involves learning to live with, and in relation to, loss" (Simon et al. 1999, 3). Loss alone, however, without sociopolitical awareness, a critical historical consciousness, and purposeful ethical activity runs the risk of rendering the possibility of healing moot before the onus of shame, guilt, resentment, fear, and hopelessness.

Santayana's (1954) plea for retentiveness of memory so as not to repeat the travesties of history, and as foothold for social progress—"those who cannot remember [or deny] the past are condemned to repeat it" (82)—only works so far as we have the power to communicate our memories, grieve, forgive, form agendas for strategic reparative action, and reconceptualize critically the way in which we live, to progress toward more universal expressions of human freedom, solidarity, and love. "Historical memory moves remembrance beyond the boundaries of the single corporal body" (Simon et al. 1999, 9) and into the general public sociopolitical and pedagogical sphere for just such a purpose.

The study of historical texts, like those encompassing the tragic events of September 11, should be a healing process, one that tightens the dialectic of human commonality. Its sociopolitical mission should find its impetus in "offering perspectives on present dilemmas and future aspirations" (3), from which ethical action for and with others should be taken. Pedagogies that expose historical trauma and engage the participants in affective intersubjective learning experiences may seem oddly apolitical. However, if taken "as strategic practice, remembrance is aligned with the anticipation of a reconciled future in which one hopes that justice and harmonious social relations might be secured" (4). This forces us to think additionally in terms of achievable moral application to the situations that confront us in our daily lives. It becomes but one of many potential vehicles by which this event and its emotional repleteness, moral enormity, and social and political complexity can be reacted to, interpreted, and retained as an inescapable and active part of our current historical landscape.

The connections between political and historical philosophy and their use in the pedagogical pursuit of ethical historical consciousness, and the necessity for critically conceived of action in our present social context, also become part of the ethical argument for this type of pedagogy. For us to ignore our circumstantial context is to perpetuate the mistakes of past action. To move forward with purpose and hope for an ethical future, we must look back: not to return to some fictional conjured version of an ideal past, but to affirm our most cherished longings for a more just and emotionally beneficial existence. We must move forward while trying to "grasp the things that are most important in the present when we turn to the past" (74), as Dewey ([1935]1963) might have it. "We move from the worse and into, not just towards, the better, which is authenticated not by comparison with the foreign but what is indigenous" (Dewey [1922]1930, 281–282) to new modes of life to be discovered, discussed, given meaning, and then fundamentally altered when the necessities of new circumstances and desires dictate.

Notes

1. See chapter 2 of Jean-Paul Sartre, *Existentialism and Human Emotions* (Secaucus, N.J.: Carol Publishing Group, 1998).
2. This is reminiscent of Kierkegaard's famous paradoxical maxim, "dread is a sympathetic antipathy and an antipathetic sympathy."

References

Buber, Martin. 1996. *I and Thou.* Translated by W. Kaufman. New York: Simon & Schuster.
Camus, Albert. [1957]1991. *The Fall.* Reprint, New York: Vintage.
Dewey, John. [1922]1930. *Human Nature and Conduct.* Reprint, New York: Modern Library.
———. [1929]1958. *Experience and Nature.* Reprint, New York: Dover.
———. [1935]1963. *Liberalism and Social Action.* Reprint, New York: Capricorn.
Greene, Maxine. 1988. *The Dialectic of Freedom.* New York: Teachers College Press.
Marcuse, Herbert. 1973. *Studies in Critical Philosophy.* Boston: Beacon.
Santayana, George. 1954. *Life of Reason.* New York: Scribners.
Simon, R. J., S. Rosenberg, and C. Eppert, eds. 1999. *Between Hope and Despair: Pedagogy and the Remembrance of Historical Trauma.* New York: Rowman & Littlefield.
Smith, Roger, ed. 1971. *Guilt: Man and Society.* New York: Anchor.
Vonnegut, Kurt. 1969. *Slaughterhouse Five.* New York: Dell.

Correspondence should be addressed to Andrew N. McKnight, 706 N. Eugene Street, Apartment B4, Greensboro, NC 27401. E-mail: anmcknight@cox.net

Teaching Cultural Studies "At a Time Like This": Reflections on Critical Pedagogy in the Wake of September 11

ANDI O'CONOR
University of Colorado at Boulder

Giroux (2002) writes that in the wake of the events of September 11, educators should facilitate "an alternative discourse grounded in a critique of militarism, consumerism, and racism" (2). In this article describes my experience teaching a university level education course in cultural studies during the aftermath of September 11. I examine the current debate about the role of cultural studies in colleges of education, and describe and discuss how the classroom became a space where students could create and participate in a critical alternative discourse.

Within the discourse of cultural studies, scholars debate both the definition and role of cultural studies, and the potentially contradictory nature of situating cultural studies within the academy (Casella 1999; Giroux 1996; Hutchinson 2000; Hytten 1999; Nelson, Treichler, and Grossberg 1992). One primary dilemma concerns the roots and history of cultural studies. While most authors locate the origins of cultural studies in Birmingham, England, others contend that cultural studies grew from various community groups and is rooted in African cultural studies (Wright 1998). As Wright states, the location of one important center of cultural studies, the Center for Contemporary Cultural Studies (CCCS) in Birmingham, England, in a university setting was problematic. He writes,

> The location of CCCS in the university was something of a double-edged sword. While it served as a strong political intervention in the academy by producing an anti-discipline, cultural studies in the University left itself open to the possibility that popular culture would in fact be examined under the academic gaze and appropriated for exclusively academic ends rather than taken up in the community in general in an involved, participatory manner. (36)

As Wright points out, calling cultural studies a discipline at all is problematic, in that it organizes and possibly reifies a field of study that is dynamic, activist, and multifaceted by nature. As Hutchinson (2000) writes, "I have a great fear that the way that cultural studies is being institutionalized in universities in the United States will no longer evoke social change. Perhaps it will engage in its inquiry and rhetoric, but it will not be a 'project'" (38). In response, Hytten, writes

> Yet I think those of us within educational departments are in a unique position to interrupt the institutionalization of an abstract and overly theoretical "discipline" of cultural studies.... If we in the academy can help these practitioners to see the world differently, and to develop critical habits of recognizing and engaging injustice, then they can bring these ideas into their own classrooms. (392)

The recent evolution of cultural studies as an academic discipline has posed particular problems for educators, activists, and newly minted professors of cultural studies. The question has been raised, Can cultural studies move forward with its activist agenda while situated in the academy? And if, as Giroux (1996) and others contend, there is a place for cultural studies in schools and colleges of Education, what might that role be? What good can come of teaching cultural studies in Education as part of an organized degree program at a university?

I believe that despite the potential hazards involved in making cultural studies a discipline within the academy, and in traditionally conservative segments of the academy such as Education, there is a powerful activist role for cultural studies to play in contemporary education programs.

Teaching Introduction to Cultural Studies in Education

In the fall of 2001, I taught a course that had recently been developed at Ohio University, Introduction to Cultural Studies in Education.[1] This was a master's level course taught as a requirement for all students getting a master's degree with a specialization in Cultural Studies in Education. The class had twenty-five students enrolled; seventeen were in-state students from Ohio, and most were classroom teachers. Half the students were getting Cultural Studies (CS) degrees, and others were specializing in a variety of areas, including special education and middle childhood education. Eight of the students were from outside the United States, from Central and South America, Sri Lanka, Japan, and Africa. I met with students for the first time on September 4, and we discussed our plans and goals for the course, and different concepts of culture. They were assigned several articles that outlined the contradictory definitions and history of CS. The topic for the next week's class, on the evening of September 11, was, "What is cultural studies?"

On the morning of September 11, my best friend called from Colorado and told me about the attacks in New York and Washington. I turned on the TV and watched in disbelief as the news showed the planes crash into the World Trade Center, over and over, the horror of it barely comprehensible. As the day wore on, I realized that the university was not canceling classes, and I would be teaching my brand-new group of graduate students that night. The dean sent an e-mail to faculty who were teaching that night, telling us it was at our discretion whether or not to hold classes. What was I going to do? Have a short discussion and send them home? Cancel class?

I walked across the street to visit with my Quaker neighbors. We watched TV together, and the three of us began to analyze and discuss the media coverage of the event. We noted how the events were already being "packaged." Within hours of the attacks, the tragedy was being labeled, similar language was being used across the networks, and logos were appearing. It seemed the discourse was already beginning to solidify; lines were quickly being drawn and enemies identified. My neighbor asked me what I was teaching that night, and I said the topic for that night's class was supposed to be "What is cultural studies?" "What a perfect opportunity!" she said. "No better time to study culture than right now, during a cultural crisis." I realized that we were engaged in cultural studies in that moment, in that living room. We were analyzing popular culture's response to a profound and political turning point in history, critically discussing what we saw, what we felt, and what it all meant. I decided to hold class.

I was still in a bit of daze when I met my class at five o'clock that night. As I entered the building, which was very quiet, I wondered if any of the students would be there. I was amazed that every single student showed up—all twenty-five of them—and some of them drove over an hour from rural locations and other nearby towns to get to class. One student asked if she could use the phone in my office down the hall to contact the airlines. One of her good friends was supposed to be on one of the planes. I left my office door open for any student who needed to make phone calls, and we came together to start class.

For the first time in my ten years of teaching college, I was at a total loss for words and had no idea how to start class. I finally said, "Well, what a day ..." and suggested that we get into groups of three and talk about the events of the day. They fanned out into the hallway, and I took some time to collect my thoughts. When we came back together, we began by listing all the words and phrases we had heard throughout the day. The board soon filled with words like, "America Under Attack," "Hunt them down," "Cowards," "Tragedy," and "Villains." Students expressed their shock, anger, hurt, and disbelief. A Muslim student from South Africa said, "My daughter was sent home from school today. Not the White kids, just the kids from other countries. My daughter said, 'Mommy they say that Muslims bombed America. But we're Muslims, and we didn't bomb anyone, did we?'"

One North American student asked, "Why is this so unreal? Why does it feel like a movie?" Many of these students were raised on disaster movies that feature some kind of catastrophic destruction of symbolic and popular structures, going all the way back to the Statue of Liberty sunk in the sand in the original *Planet of the Apes*. One student said angrily, "We're supposed to *wake up* from this. The lights are supposed to come on and we're supposed to go HOME. It's not supposed to be REAL." We discussed what it means to grow up in a cinematic culture, where disasters are seen as entertainment. At this point, a student from Sri Lanka joined the discussion. "No disrespect intended," she said, "but for those of us in this room who grew up with terrorism and murder as 'normal' happenings, we do not see this as cinema. This is too much like real life." The domestic students were silent, and listened as she described the horrors of decades of civil war in Sri Lanka.

The discussion became uncomfortable at times, especially since these students had only known each other for a week. A student from Central America said, "I keep hearing the word 'cowards' when referring to the attackers. Why do these American journalists think it is cowardly for one small nation to attack the most powerful country in the world? To sacrifice your life in the process, this is cowardly?" "Well," replied one domestic student, "I think they *are* cowards and I *do* want to hunt them down and kill them. I'm sorry, but I do." I asked them to think about why the United States would be perceived as an enemy worthy of attack. A student from Central America said, "I'm not excusing what happened, but the U.S. policy of 'free trade' is killing people in developing countries. You ask why they attacked the Trade Centers and Pentagon—it seems to me like a clear statement against U.S. military policies and free trade. Why else choose these targets?" One student asked, "Why did they keep showing the picture of the Twin Towers falling over and over again? I must have seen that scene a hundred times today! Why didn't they show the Pentagon as much? Why didn't they show many of the people who were hurt? It was just the Towers, the buildings, over and over again." Said one, "It's because in America, money is more important than government." Said another, "It's because so many more lives were lost in New York." Another replied bitterly, "It was better television."

We discussed cultural studies and the media and the importance of television in particular for the production and distribution of cultural forms. One student said, "Well, what I'm learning tonight is that these guys [television producers] are really playing on my feelings. I feel like I'm being told how to feel. I'm supposed to be angry at a certain person. I'm supposed to start hating Arabs. I'm supposed to suspect anyone who's brown or Muslim. It's making me mad." Another added, "How come everyone has the same headline on their newscasts now? It only happened this morning, and all the stations say 'Attack on America.' Do they call each other and decide this stuff, or what? People are dead and they're wondering what to *call* it?"

"It's a national emergency," replied another student. "The president is doing his best, the media is doing their best. It's our job as Americans to support the president, and to help people who need help." One student from Central America asked, "Well, then what's my job? My North American guy roommates told me this was 'none of my business' because I'm not 'American.' I am too American! I'm just not *North* American! They said, 'Don't worry, we'll take care of this. This doesn't concern you.' Doesn't concern me? How is that possible?" One of the domestic students said, "I know it's a national emergency, but isn't it also our job as cultural studies students, and as educators, to question the actions of our government? Shouldn't we all go back to our classrooms tomorrow morning and talk about this stuff critically?" "No, not with my kids," said another student. "I'm just going to tell them I love them and that everything will be okay, and then go on with my lesson plan." "What am I going to tell my special ed kids tomorrow?" asked another. "Today the principal ordered us not to talk about it with the kids—we just sent them home."

At the end of class I added, "This is cultural production in action. Let's all watch out for what's being produced here—what kind of symbols and language, who becomes the 'good guys' and the 'bad guys.' For the next week, pay close attention to the media coverage, and be ready to talk about it in light of the readings."

After three hours I dismissed class, and many students stayed after to continue the discussion. After everyone left, I sat in the empty classroom for a long time, copying the notes we had written on the board, and writing down everything I remembered the students saying. I was exhausted, and also filled with a profound sense of gratitude for my role as a professor of cultural studies. I didn't have to abandon my curriculum to talk about the events of the day—the day became the "lesson plan." The classroom that night had been a place where we could openly discuss the profound events of the day, to begin, as Giroux (2002, 2) advocates, to provide an alternative discourse "that is grounded in a critique of militarism, consumerism, and racism," and challenges the "retrograde appeal to jingoistic patriotism" (?). I decided to continue documenting the discussions in this class, as I had a sense that it would provide a window into an important and historical moment in my own teaching history, as well as enlighten me on some basic issues about the function of cultural studies in education.

The next week, as soon as class started, one of the students said, "Okay, we have to talk about this ribbon thing. Why did the ribbons start out being white, and then change to red, white, and blue?" Another student replied, "It's a sign of support—for the country, for the people who were lost, for the rescue workers. It's patriotic, it's good. It means we're all together—we're united. Like we're united against AIDS, and breast cancer." We discussed the importance of cultural symbols, like ribbons, flag emblems, and T-shirts. "I love wearing the flag and flying the flag," said another North American student. "It means I support my country, I support freedom and all the things people are trying to take from me by attacking America." An international student responded, "How is that possible? How can anyone take anything from Americans? To me the American flag is a sign of world domination, of the most super of the superpowers. It means, 'We are the strongest. We are the best. We do whatever we want because we have the most power.' That's why it is burned in other parts of the world, to protest this."

Throughout the class meetings, the subject invariably came back to the events of September 11. As we discussed culture, power, the history and applications of cultural studies, its relevance to education, feminism, critical race studies, and other topics, the discussion always came back to the coverage of the events, the military mobilization, and the public rhetoric. When discussing semiotics in a group presentation, one student brought in a large copy of a *Time* magazine cover that featured President George W. Bush on top of a hill of rubble at Ground Zero, surrounded by rescue workers, with a large American flag prominently featured. The student guided the class in a semiotic analysis of the photo, showing how to more deeply analyze media images.

Giroux (1996, 45) writes that educators, particularly in cultural studies, need to expand the curricula "to allow students to become critically literate in those visual, electronic, and digital cultures that have such an important influence on their lives," and to teach students to be "cultural producers" as well. I realized that because of September 11, this class would not be just a theoretical examination of cultural studies in Education, or a way to relate cultural studies to educational practices. Since the focus of so much of our day-to-day lives was the aftermath of September 11, it became a necessary core of the curriculum. And since so much of the impact was being constructed and conveyed through the media, the class became, in a sense, a course on critical media literacy, in the expanded form that Giroux discusses above. Students, through their group work, discussion, and presentation of cultural artifacts, were becoming cultural producers as well as consumers.

As the term progressed, the students began to bring critical questions about the media representations of events surrounding September 11 for the class to discuss. During one class, students were discussing the television tribute on the show *Saturday Night Live* that featured Mayor Rudolph Guiliani and a host of rescue workers, arranged on stage in full rescue gear and uniforms, while Paul Simon sang "An American Tune." One student noted, "Did you guys notice that there were no women on that stage? Not anywhere! And no black firefighters or police officers. All except two were White, and they looked Latino, maybe." Another said, "Well, it's not just *Saturday Night Live.* How many pictures of women and blacks have you seen in the paper? On the news? What about that picture of the guys holding up the flag at Ground Zero? Aren't they all White males?" I asked how that might impact them as educators. One replied, "Well, it's our job to counteract that image. Talk about it with our kids. Tell them that yes, there are Black and women firefighters and police officers and rescue workers. The women aren't just in the back cooking for the fire*men.*" Another laughed and said, "Oh, it's like revisionist history! The new history textbooks are going to show all White men firefighters, and we're going to be the ones for years going, 'No, there really were women there that day. No, people of color did play a role in the rescue. No, the brown people weren't just the bad guys that day. We have to be like Howard Zinn and tell the story from another point of view."

"Who's going to tell this story anyway?" asked another. "Who gets to write it in the textbooks in the first place? Can't we figure out a way to influence that? We're teachers, we use textbooks every day. Don't we have a say?" We then began to discuss how histories are written, contested, and rewritten, and the policies and politics of textbook publication.

We often began class with an open discussion about our experiences of the week. One evening, a student said, "Here's my favorite new thing that I'm hearing on TV and reading in the paper. 'Since September 11, there is no more race in America. No African Americans, no Hispanic Americans, no Asian Americans. We're all just Americans!' And they showed a young Black kid saying this! What is up with *that?* And overnight, racism is gone? Black men are no longer the majority in prison? Housing and job discrimination have disappeared? Women now make the same as men? What are people thinking when they say stuff like this?"

He was outraged at how race was being "disappeared" in the wake of September 11. I shared that I had an experience while en route to a conference in October, when an affluent-looking White businessman seated next to me made an almost identical statement. He said, "But you know what's great about all this? There's no more race in America! We're all just Americans!" It turned out that our flight was delayed because the only person of color on the small commuter flight, an English professor of East Indian descent, had been pulled out of line, taken to a room, and strip-searched. No more race in America, indeed.

On the same trip, I changed planes in Cincinnati and stopped at an information kiosk staffed by two volunteers. A very sweet woman, who looked about sixty-five, helped me locate my gate on a map. She wore a vest that was covered with American flag buttons, ribbons, and jewelry, and wore a red, white, and blue hat with tiny flags stuck all around the brim. As I was turning to leave, she reached over to a stack of American flag stickers and tried to hand one to me. "Have a sticker, it's for your coat," she said cheerily. I said, "Oh, no thank you, I don't want a flag sticker, but thanks anyway, and thanks for your help." Her face instantly changed to a scowl, and she nearly shouted, "You don't want a *sticker?* Don't you know what this STANDS for?" "Yes, I do know what it stands for," I replied calmly, "and I don't choose to show my patriotism by wearing a flag." She glared angrily as I walked away. Clearly I had upset this woman, who was giving her time to help travelers in the airport. But I was also tired of the assumption that everyone, particularly a nicely dressed, professional-looking White woman like myself, would want to wear a flag sticker.

I explained to the students that I was frustrated with the commodification of the September 11 tragedy in flag stickers, car flags, pins, T-shirts, and posters, and that I was tired of what I considered rampant uncritical nationalism that was sweeping the country. "That's it!" replied one student. "That's the phrase I've been looking for, to describe what's been bothering me. 'Rampant uncritical nationalism.'"

As the weeks passed and we continued our exploration of cultural studies and education, the discussion continued to center around the events of September 11. It was a constant reference point and point of relevance for students. Several students brought in antiwar Web sites, articles, and information. And many students continued to speak out in defense of U.S. policies and practices in Afghanistan and domestically. The discussion was lively, and rarely antagonistic, except for a few frustrated outbursts from both "sides" from time to time. I wondered at this and surmised that coming together as a class on September 11 had served as a bonding experience for these students, regardless of how they felt about the political nature of the events of the day.

At the end of the term, students reflected on their experiences, through presentations and in their final papers. One North American student, whose friend died in New York on September 11, wrote that her thinking had changed throughout the course. She said,

> When this all started I was just angry—at bin Laden, at Afghanistan. I wanted to bomb them all to hell. But all fall we've been discussing what's going on underneath the media hype. Now I wonder, is retaliation the best thing? Are there things we do as a country that we should change? And what can I do to help change them?

Wrote another, "As educators and/or educational advocates, it is our job to critically evaluate the artifacts that popular culture presents to us." It seems that some students had begun to take steps toward becoming critical evaluators of not only popular culture, but of the deeper policies and practices that are expressed through popular culture, and particularly through the media.

Looking back on the class, I continue to ponder the questions raised by Hutchinson, Giroux, Hytten, and others. I have long believed, as hooks (1994) writes, that teaching can be a profoundly transformative act, and that the classroom can be a "radical space of possibility." Yet, as Hutchinson queries (2002, 386), given the radical and transformative nature of cultural studies, and the potential of cultural studies in education, "Is it enough?" Is it enough to provide a space within academe to question the cultural production and distribution of knowledge, without a specific agenda of intervention? Does intellectual exploration of these issues change anything? Do cultural studies classes like this one promote genuine social change, or are classes like these merely exercises in discourse and pedagogy?

Apparently, at this moment in time, alternative discourse is being seen, at least by some, as a truly radical act, and as threatening the very foundation of "American civilization." According to The American Council of Trustees and Alumni (ACTA) report, "Defending Civilization: How Our Universities are Failing America and What Can be Done About It," academics around the country who have challenged or questioned U.S. policies since September 11 have been voicing "explicit condemnations of America" (1).[2] The ACTA report claims,

> While America's elected officials from both parties and media commentators from across the spectrum condemned the attacks and followed the President in calling evil by its rightful name, many faculty demurred. Some refused to make judgments. Many invoked tolerance and diversity as antidotes to evil. Some even pointed accusatory fingers, not at the terrorists, but at America itself. (1)

One quote included in the ACTA report was from an unnamed professor of Art at the University of North Carolina, who allegedly said, "We offer this teach-in as an alternative to the cries of war as an end to the cycle of continued global violence" (12). Apparently, the ACTA and its supporters consider holding a teach-in (conducting a free educational event for the general public) an unpatriotic act of subversion. Another objectionable quote was from a professor of Anthropology at Massachusetts Institute of Technology, who said,

> Imagine the real suffering and grief of people in other countries. The best way to begin a war on terrorism might be to look in the mirror. (2)

Another activity the ACTA found objectionable was the behavior of University of California at Berkeley students at a rally, who chanted, "Stop the violence—stop the hate" (example #110, 28).

The report lauds more "responsible" statements that "leaders from both parties" have made. They quote Mayor Rudolph Giuliani, who said, "On one side is democracy, the rule of law, and respect for human life; on the other is tyranny, arbitrary executions, and mass murder. We're right and they're wrong. It's as simple as that" (2).

The report goes on to list over a hundred quotes by unnamed academics (taken almost exclusively from newspaper articles and Web sites) who did not "follow the President by calling evil by its name" but questioned the rhetoric around the events of September 11. As the report states, "The message from much of academe was BLAME AMERICA FIRST" (3) The implicit message from the ACTA is that any questioning of the long and contested history of U.S. foreign policy, that any disagreement with the president, that digression from the party line of "we're right and they're wrong. It's as simple as that" borders on, if not is, an act of subversion.

According to Lynne Cheney, the co-founder of ACTA, when universities added new courses in response to September 11, this was somehow just another way of "blaming America" for the tragedy. She said, in a speech on October 5, 2001, "To say that it is more important now [to study Islam] implies that the events of September 11 were our fault, that it was our failure ... that led to so many deaths and so much destruction" (Martin and Neal 2001, 6). Apparently, even creating an expanded space for discussion on Islam or other critical topics poses a threat to the "good of the nation," and should be avoided at all costs.

Some academics quoted in the report were surprised that their bringing up the subject in classes would make such an impact on the ACTA. Rob Loftis, who teaches Philosophy at Auburn University, wrote that he argued in class against the bombing of Afghanistan.

> I made similar remarks in the classes I teach, and I also spoke out against the violations of civil liberties that the war effort has brought. For some reason, my attempts to corrupt the youth of America and undermine the war effort failed, and the United States began bombing Afghanistan in short order. Nevertheless, my efforts were clearly unpatriotic, and I deserve to be on any enemies list compiled by ACTA, or whoever Joe McCarthy's successors are today. (Sherwin 2002, 1)

Martin Sherwin (2002), a professor of English and American History at Tufts University, placed an ad in the magazine *The Nation,* inviting faculty members who might have made statements offensive to the ACTA to "come forward" and name themselves. The responses were placed on *The Nation* Web site, under the title, "Tattletales for an Open Society." So far, over a hundred people have responded, including professors, adjunct instructors, and public school teachers. As one wrote, "Not only do Cheney and Lieberman want us to prejudge the situation ('Bush is right, all doubters wrong'), they are actively seeking to silence dissent. Those who love freedom, whatever they think of this war, should not allow themselves to be cowed. James P. Levy, Adjunct Assistant Professor of History, Hofstra University" (Sherwin, 6) Wrote another,

I want to alert ACTA that—though they have appointed themselves to monitor faculty and alumni there are many itinerant agitators on American campuses. I occasionally teach and lecture on college campuses and have made a number of statements in recent months about the immorality and hypocrisy of our current military aggression. ... I'm very likely to do this again in lectures and classes this spring. Please don't limit your organization's venue to those privileged to hold tenure or academic appointments, but keep an eye on other intellectuals, scholars, activists and artists in our communities. (Sallie Tisdale, writer, Portland, Oregon, cited in Sherman 2002, 6)

Daniel D. Fineman, a professor at Occidental College, summed up the debate eloquently, and wrote, "The only appropriate response to this terrorism is to engage vibrantly the difficult issues and conditions that led to 9–11, to encourage, not stigmatize, debate and diversity of opinion. Let us not make our defense our defeat."

At a time when academic critique of military and political decisions is being criticized with a McCarthy-like zeal, I feel privileged to have experienced a space within academe, created and sustained largely by the students, in which military policies, media representation of current events, as well as implications for race and gender politics could be openly discussed. Each week, the students opened new avenues of discussion that made the classroom a place of contestation and potential transformation. And yet I still wonder, is it enough?

Is it enough that students had a space to question, even though, to my knowledge, most took no concrete action to protest the military response or the media coverage of the post–September 11 events? Did the curriculum and practice of cultural studies in education live up to its performative, or as Hutchinson writes (2002, 382–390), its "distributive" potential? Or is the dialog itself, as Hytten (2000) claims, the precursor to an activism that an instructor may never see? I'm not sure what will happen in the long run. It is perhaps not enough, but, rather, a beginning.

Postscript

Now it's January of 2002, and I'm teaching undergraduate Foundations of Education and a doctoral level course, Critical Theories of Education. We're studying testing and tracking, history of education, and social context issues, and talking about radical theoretical frameworks. Although the military actions in Afghanistan continue, the events of September 11 have yet to come up in class. It's as if, over the winter break, the students took a vacation from the trauma and challenge of these events and decided not to come back. The captions on television these days read, "America Seeks Justice." I'm not teaching any master's degree students this term, so I haven't seen many of the students from last fall's class. I wonder about my former cultural studies students. Are they tired of analyzing the issues? Are they back to "business as usual," in their own classrooms, in their graduate classes at the university? And again I ask myself, in times like these, Is it enough?

Notes

1. This course was initially developed by Dr. Jaylynne Hutchinson, and I am grateful for her help and guidance with the syllabus.
2. ACTA has also launched the Defense of Civilization Fund, which will be used to "support and defend the study of American history and civics and of Western civilization" (Martin and Neal 2001, 1). See the American Council of Trustees and Alumni home page, http://www.goacta.org/

References

American Council of Trustees and Alumni. 2001. Home page, http://www.goacta.org/

Casella, Ronnie. 1999. "What are we doing when we are 'doing' Cultural Studies in Education — and Why?" *Educational Theory*, 49 (1): 107–123.

Chronicle of Higher Education. 2002 (January 25). "A glance at the Web site of 'The Nation': Professors turn themselves in for comments about the war." Retrieved on January 25, 2002, from www.Chronicle.com

Giroux, Henry. 1996. "Is there a place for Cultural Studies in Colleges of Education?" In *Counternarratives: Cultural Studies and Critical Pedagogies in Postmodern Spaces.* Edited by C. Lankshear, Peter McLaren, and Michael Peters. New York: Routlege.

———. 2002. "Democracy, Freedom and Justice after September 11th: Rethinking the Role of Educators and the Politics of Schooling." Teacher's College Record online, retrieved on January 26, 2002, from www.tcrecord.org

hooks, bell. 1994. *Teaching to Transgress: Education as the Practice of Freedom.* New York: Routledge.

Hutchinson, Jaylynne. 2000. "A Queasy Scholar Considers Cultural Studies." *Philosophy of Education 2000.* Philosophy of Education Society, University of Illinois at Urbana-Champaign, Urbana, IL.

Hytten, Kathy. 1999. "The Promise of Cultural Studies of Education." *Educational Theory* 49 (4): 124–126.

———. 2000. "On the Importance of Being Queasy." *Philosophy of Education 2000.* Philosophy of Education Society, University of Illinois at Urbana-Champaign, Urbana, IL.

Martin, J., and A. Neal. 2001 (November). "Defending Civilization: How Our Universities are Failing America and What Can be Done About It." A Project of the Defense of Civilization Fund. American Council of Trustees and Alumni. Retrieved on January 26, 2002, from http://www.goacta.org/Reports/defciv.pdf

Nelson, C., Paul Treichler, and Lawrence Grossberg. 1992. *Cultural Studies.* New York: Routledge.

Sherwin, Martin J. 2002. "Tattletales for an Open Society." *The Nation* Web site, retrieved on January 26, 2002, from http://www.thenation.com The Nation Company, L.P.

Wright, Handel K. 1998. "Dare We De-Centre Birmingham? Troubling The Origin and Trajectories Of Cultural Studies." *European Journal of Cultural Studies* 1:33–56.

Correspondence should be addressed to Andi O'Conor, University of Colorado at Boulder, School of Education, Box 249, Boulder, CO 80309. E-mail: andi.oconor@colorado.edu

POETRY

perhaps we should actually talk ...

CHRISTOPHER KNAUS
University of Washington

The great talking circle
talking around the perimeter of racism
hammering around the heart of the issue
surfacing so clearly, so silently
   the privilege of language:
   "Return to normalcy"
normality?
   Who can return?
Racism gets pointed out, however harshly
   to white people and BAM! We
   can't let this impact us—
   SHOW NO REMORSE, do not
   back down—we will prevail and
"we" becomes white
   and normal is racist
and so where does that leave
people of color?

Mental health "experts" say what kids need is to
return to normalcy in the face of Sept. 11th
but I think of Afghani kids and how
they return to the normality of death from starvation or from american bombs

americans, we must return to the luxurious normality of vainly hidden hate
we must protect our adults who can't conceive of changing our lives, who can't
conceive of the global impact of our capitalistic consumerist culture built and
maintained upon slavery;
This is not about our kids.
   white patriarchal mental health "experts"

defenders of blatant ignorance:
let's let our kids decide how to respond to the terrorism that maintains the middle
class
let's let our young scholars decide rather than let us continue to hide.

TIME EXPOSURE

The Woodcock-Johnson® is among the most widely used diagnostic tests in education. The purpose of the test is to measure both cognitive ability and achievement in children. The test uses a number of methods to determine the level of subjects, including picture identification items. In Test 4 of the Achievement section, subjects are asked to identify different items and activities going on in the picture of a park with buildings in the background. The image includes children playing, people exercising, and so on. A plane flies across the top of the picture in the direction of two skyscrapers. Following the terrorist attack on the World Trade Center on September 11, 2001, the image has become particularly haunting.

Children taking the test have suddenly become very sensitive to the content of the picture. One colleague was recently using the test with a young child who asked, "Why are you showing me this picture?" The item has been revised by the Riverside Publishing Company, the publisher of the test. The plane now flies away from the downtown area. There is now a single skyscraper where there had been two before. The revision of the test item suggests how images used in educational and testing materials can take on profoundly new meanings in light of current events.

Riverside Publishing has asked us not to use the image of the test item, or to describe it in too much detail. They explained that to do so might jeopardize the validity of the item. We have honored their request and substituted a memorial.

Additional materials in this series can be found at the Time Exposures Web site:
Visual Explorations in the History of American Education
http://www.education.miami.edu/ep/TimeExposures/

EUGENE F. PROVENZO, JR.
University of Miami

At 08:48 Eastern Daylight Time American Airlines Flight 11 crashes into the north tower of New York's World Trade Center. Eighteen minutes later United Airlines Flight 175 crashes into the south tower.

The Memory of 9/11

Eulogy for Professor G. Max Wingo

Those of us who work within the various academic fields and modes of inquiry that constitute Social/Cultural Foundations of Education and Educational Studies are a somewhat unique community of teacher-scholars in teacher education. The interpretive, critical, and normative nature of our pedagogical and scholarly work has caused, in many instances, colleagues and students to be uncomfortable with, and sometimes even suspicious of or hostile to, our approaches to teacher education. In these times of renewed efforts to make schooling and education more responsive to the imperatives of capitalism and the class State(s), our community members have provided some of the best arguments in opposition to these powerful demands. We in the foundations of education and educational studies have done much of the heavy lifting that is necessary to strengthen the democratic imperative on schools, colleges, and universities in the United States. Because of the comparative smallness of our community, and due to the critical work that we do, it is important for us to keep in mind what our traditions are and have been. In addition to the need for cooperation and solidarity among us with regard to key problems and possibilities facing school and society, I argue further that we must remember those who helped construct this field in which we work. In this eulogy I honor Max Wingo, who died on September 14, 2001, in Ann Arbor, Michigan.

The following is taken from the obituary in the *Ann Arbor News*.

> Professor Wingo was born in Fair Grove, Missouri, in 1913. He earned a B.Sc. degree from Southwest Missouri State Teachers College in 1933, an M.A. from Columbia in 1938, and a Ph.D. at Yale in 1941. He taught in the public schools in Springfield, Missouri, and served as an elementary principal in Darien, Connecticut, before joining the faculty at Michigan in 1945. At Michigan's School of Education, he was principal of University Elementary School and director of elementary teacher training. He became full professor in 1954, teaching core courses in the philosophy and history of education, as well as serving on many doctoral committees.

The newspaper writer tells us that Wingo's broad knowledge and keen interest in science and the humanities, along with his dry wit, helped provide family, friends, and students with insightful perspectives on the human experience. Max Wingo was the author of many journal articles and books.

I have known "Max" Wingo since being a student in his Philosophy of Education class during my master's work in 1961–1962. To my knowledge, students never called him "Max" at that time; moreover, this was the case when I returned to Ann Arbor to work on a doctorate "under" him. In fact, I never called him "Max" until 1999 when I met him for brunch after a football game. During the late 1990s, he had agreed to read the manuscript that I was working on; therefore, we exchanged ideas about the work on a continuous basis. It seemed time to move beyond my former letter correspondence with him over the years between 1972 and this time of collegial correspondence about the book project. Up until the late 1990s correspondence, my letters to him featured greetings such as "Dear Maestro," "Dear GMW," with an occasional "Dear Dr. Wingo." I mention this because of the complex ways I experienced this very good person and classic professor. Others who knew him understand well that Wingo was the kind of man who commanded one's respect because of the work that he did, the way he presented himself in class and in his office, as well as the sense students had that we could trust this teacher-scholar to help us develop the project(s) that had brought us to Michigan's School of Education in the first place. When I finally was courageous enough at the brunch during the autumn of 1999 to suggest we talk about "what I should address him as," he replied, "Why not Max?"

Perhaps I'm the only one who experienced Max Wingo as a Bogart-like figure—at least the actor at his best in certain Casablanca scenes. He smoked Camel cigarettes with style; his wit was dry and ironic; his kindness was underlined by a resolute commitment to calling things by their right names; he was never condescending toward students, treating us instead as being capable of accomplishing what we stated as our goals; and finally, his intelligence served to make clear that he could see through artifice.

When I was a master's student, it seemed to me that Wingo was teaching from his notes. In my experience, this was typical of most of the professors in the Literature, Science, and Arts College at Michigan during that time. When I returned in 1970, his book, *The Philosophy of American Education,* was available. It was clear that this classic book had emerged from Wingo's studies and teaching and, specifically, his notes. This accomplishment was one among many others in his scholarly, pedagogic, and mentor career.

Max Wingo knew that philosophers of education should never forget that our work must ultimately be "useful" to those who are responsible for teaching and learning. He was, of course, very committed to the parent discipline of philosophy qua philosophy. Although he never doubted that philosophy was inextricably one with both formal and informal educational endeavors, he criticized those persons in teacher education who allegedly "did not know the front from the back of a schoolhouse." His own involvement with teaching and learning in the schools provided some of the most important perspectives through which he viewed philosophical inquiry. I believe that he also viewed philosophy of education as belonging within social foundations of education contexts. This school and society approach to teacher education helped ensure that philosophy of education would be grounded in the concreteness of everyday life in both sites.

Maestro Wingo always presented the various philosophies and philosophies of education clearly, fairly, and eloquently. This occurred verbally and via his elegant prose style. One could understand the various "isms" (e.g., essentialism, idealism, realism, progressivism, pragmatism, Marxism, existentialism, perennialism, etc.) as discussed by Wingo almost as if the respective spokespersons were addressing you. He made clear that if one were to adopt the various philosophers' underlying assumptions, then their political, economic, social, and educational positions also made logical sense. This is not to claim that the interested listener, dialoguer, or reader would have difficulty discerning what Professor Wingo's preferences were and why. His admiration for liberalism, pragmatist philosophy, and educational progressivism was kept in tension by his keen intelligence, "street smarts," inquisitiveness, and skepticism.

One could always use Wingo's presentations to go beyond the specifics of what he said and wrote because he was an open-ended thinker. His commitment to, and understanding of, experimental science served to make him respectful of tentativeness and "warranted assertibility." In this way he had much in common with John Dewey. Many have argued that Dewey's liberalism helped change what that term and position meant. Furthermore, it provided possibilities for more radical assessments of school and society. My experiences with Wingo encouraged me to think, write, and teach "beyond" the analyses he provided—as well as his own, understated, core beliefs. I think this is the case for many of his other students. Obviously "beyond" does not mean better. Dr. Wingo never tried to develop "followers" out of his students or colleagues. His goal as a teacher-scholar and colleague was to present clear arguments, explanations, and underlying assumptions that were aimed at making dialogue and understanding more possible.

I used Wingo's writings in my graduate Philosophy of Education classes at Ball State University. Many of the students agreed with me that one indication of the classic nature of his prose was that it was almost impossible to rewrite more clearly what he had written. The students were impressed also by the enduring nature of his work even as we were all subjected, during the last third of the twentieth century, to what Marx called the melting of everything that seemed solid into air. My students were favorably impressed, too, by Max's dedication in his Philosophy of Education books: "To Mary [my wife and professional colleague], who spends her days in the schools doing the things her husband mostly talks about." I always reminded them that Max had been the principal of the University of Michigan Elementary School when he first came to Ann Arbor and that what he was doing in Philosophy of Education was also worthwhile and "practical."

Here are some examples of Wingo's ideas in print.

> If progressive education is to have a future it had better forego any temptation to make itself into a kind of pseudo-theology, as some say it has already done. It had better stick to its historic allegiance to empirical inquiry, scientific evidence, and the moral conviction that democracy offers a common ground on which the good life can be defined and achieved by all—regardless of metaphysical differences. If the history of philosophy shows anything, it shows that if we must wait for educational progress until we get our metaphysics straightened out and agreed on, we are going to have a great deal of time on our hands. (Wingo 1956, 21)

> In the times immediately ahead it will be necessary to reappraise and, in many ways, to redefine both the aims and the means of education.... I am convinced that much of what has been done by educational conservatives in the past two decades [mutatis mutandis from 1965 through the present] will be seen in historical perspective as not much more than a delaying action, designed to postpone as long as possible the inevitable confrontation with the changed condition of the new age. Certainly, it will be unfortunate, and possibly disastrous, if we continue to think of the major problems of educational policy as being whether team teaching is superior to the self-contained classroom or whether teaching machines are superior to flesh-and-blood teachers.... We already have some reasonably good techniques for assessing the effectiveness of different educational techniques. As yet, we have not shown ourselves very able at discerning what ends are relevant to the conditions of life in a society that is being transformed. (Wingo 1965, 433)

> In educational method, the general approach to instructional problems is ... [to] reorganize. Proposals for achieving this are well known, even to the general public: ungraded classrooms, team teaching, performance objectives, schools without walls, and not least, the various programs based on educational technology. Accompanying these changes in structural organization are efforts at reorganizing curricula and curriculum materials. For the most part, these developments have followed the traditional subject matter lines that have been the mainstay of conservative educational policy for decades. (Wingo 1974, 345)

> It is appropriate to point out here that amid all the myriad activities directed at the rehabilitation of education, the claims and counterclaims, the organizing and reorganizing, and the researching and developing, not to mention the proliferation of gadgetry, one question was rarely raised, if ever. Yet this question is strategic beyond all others. It can be asked in deceptively simple language, but we know

from the inquiry we have made in our consideration of the individual philosophies how complicated the question is and how fateful the answer given to it can
be. The question is, What are the purposes education should serve? Or more simply, What is teaching for? (Wingo 1974, 345)

Max Wingo shall be missed. Those who know his work can still make it known
to those who have not yet enjoyed the "pleasure of his company."

RICHARD A. BROSIO
University of Wisconsin at Milwaukee

References

Wingo, G. Max. 1956. "The Future of Progressive Education." *The University of Michigan
School of Education Bulletin* 25 (2): 17–21.
———. 1965. *The Philosophy of American Education.* Lexington, Mass.: Heath.
———. 1974. *Philosophies of Education: An Introduction.* Lexington, Mass.: Heath.

BOOKS AVAILABLE LIST

BOOKS RECEIVED WINTER 2002

Berube, Maurice R. *Beyond Modernism and Postmodernism: Essays on the Politics of Culture.* Westport, Conn.: Greenwood, 2002. pp. 160. $56.00 (cloth).

Bracey, Earnest N. *Prophetic Insight: The Higher Education and Pedagogy of African Americans.* Lanham, Md.: University Press of America, 1999. pp.143. $29.97 (cloth), $13.25 (paper).

Cole, Ardra L., and J. Gary Knowles. *Lives in Context: The Art of Life History Research.* Walnut Creek, Calif.: AltaMira Press, 2001. pp. 272. $62.00 (cloth), $22.95 (paper).

Crotty, Michael. *The Foundations of Social Research: Meaning and Perspective in the Research Process.* London, England: Sage, 1998. pp. 248. $27.95 (cloth).

Edwards, June. *Women in American Education, 1820–1955: The Female Force and Educational Reform.* Westport, Conn.: Greenwood, 2001. pp. 176. $55.00 (cloth).

Form, William. *Work and Academic Politics: A Journeyman's Story.* New Brunswick, N.J.: Transaction Publications, 2002. pp. 247. $34.95 (cloth).

Gill, Brian P., P. Michael Timpane, Karen E. Ross, and Dominic J. Brewer. *Rhetoric Versus Reality: What We Know and What We Need to Know About Vouchers and Charter Schools.* Santa Monica, Calif.: RAND, 2001. pp. 290. $15.00 (paper).

Gregory, Sheila T. *Black Women in the Academy: The Secrets to Success and Achievement.* Lanham, Md.: University Press of America, 1999. pp. 213. Price NA (cloth), $27.50 (paper).

Guerrero-Avila, Juan B. *Hispanic Experience in Higher Education: Mexican Southern Baptists' Attitudes Toward Higher Education.* Lanham, Md.: University Press of America, 1999. pp. 120. $29.00 (cloth).

Hoggart, Richard. *Between Two Worlds: Politics, Anti-Politics, and the Unpolitical.* New Brunswick, N.J.: Transaction, 2002. pp. 313. $39.95 (cloth).

Holst, John D. *Social Movements, Civil Society, and Radical Adult Education.* Westport, Conn.: Greenwood, 2001. pp. 176. $50.00 (cloth).

Horowitz, Tamar. *Children of Perestroika in Israel.* Lanham, Md.: University Press of America, 1999. pp. 227. $28.50 (cloth).

Kahler, Dan. *Successful Schools: Achieving Escellence Through Star Theory.* Lanham, Md.: Scarecrow Press, 2002. pp.168. $26.95 (paper).

Kirby, Sheila Nataraj, Mark Berends, and Scott Naftel. *Implementation in a Longitudinal Sample of New American Schools: Four Years into Scale-Up.* Santa Monica, Calif.: RAND, 2001. pp. 99. $15.00 (cloth).

Levin, Claudia. *Only a Teacher: Three Part Video Documentary.* Boston: McGraw-Hill Higher Education, 2002. Price NA.

Manning, Kathleen. *Giving Voice to Critical Campus Issues: Qualitative Research in Student Affairs.* Lanham, Md.: University Press of America, 1999. pp. 146. $53.00 (cloth).

McCarty, Teresa. *A Place to be Navajo: Rough Rock and the Struggle for Self-Determination in Indigenous Schooling.* Mahwah, N.J.: Lawrence Erlbaum Associates, Inc., 2002. pp. 229. $24.95 (paper).

McClellan, B. Edward. *Moral Education in America: Schools and the Shaping of Character from Colonial Times to Present.* New York: Teachers College Press,1999. pp. 130. $21.95 (paper).

Meyer, Richard J. *Phonics Exposed: Understanding and Resisting Systematic Direct Intense Phonics Instruction.* Mahwah, N.J.: Lawrence Erlbaum Associates, Inc., 2002. pp. 180 $45.00 (paper).

Mitchell, Samuel. *Effective Educational Partnerships: Experts, Advocates, and Scouts.* Westport, Conn.: Praeger, 2002. pp. 272 $67.95 (cloth).

Nash, Robert J. *Religious Pluralism in the Academy: Opening the Dialogue.* New York: Peter Lang, 2001. pp. 232. $29.95 (paper).

Osborn, Terry A. *The Future of Foreign Language Education in the United States.* Westport, Conn.: Bergin & Garvey, 2002. pp. 192. $59.95 (cloth).

Podeh, Elie. *The Arab-Israeli Conflict in Israeli History Textbooks, 1948–2000.* Westport, Conn.: Bergin & Garvey, 2002. pp. 216. $58.00 (cloth).

Post, David. *Children's Work, Schooling, and Welfare in Latin America.* Boulder, Colo.: Westview, 2002. pp.284. $35.00 (paper).

Reagan, Timothy G., and Terry A. Osborn. *The Foreign Language Educator in Society: Toward a Critical Pedagogy.* Mahwah, N.J.: Lawrence Erlbaum Associates, Inc., 2002. pp. 185. $24.50 (paper).

Rosenfeld, Jona M., and Bruno Tardieu. *Artisans of Democracy: How Ordinary People, Families in Extreme Poverty, and Social Institutions Become Allies to Overcome Social Exclusion.* Lanham, Md.: University Press of America, 2000. pp. 276. $52.00 (paper).

Salmon, Diane, and Ruth Ann Freedman. *Facilitating Interpersonal Relationships in the Classroom: The Relational Literacy Curriculum.* Mahwah, N.J.: Lawrence Erlbaum Associates, Inc., 2002. pp. 178. $22.50 (paper).

Schramm, Susan L. *Transforming the Curriculum: Thinking Outside the Box.* Lanham, Md.: Scarecrow Education Press, 2002. pp. 90. $19.95 (paper).

Sirotnik, Kenneth A., and Roger Soder. *The Beat of a Different Drummer: Essays on Educational Renewal in Honor of John I. Goodlad.* New York: Peter Lang, 1999. pp. 318. $24.95 (paper).

Smith, William A., Philip G. Altbach, and Kofi Lomotey. *The Racial Crisis in American Higher Education: Continuing Challenges for the Twenty-first Century,* rev. ed. Albany: State University of New York Press, 2002. pp. 313. $51.83 (cloth).

Upshur-Ransome, Cora Lee. *A Comparison of the African-American Presence in an Earlier and Later American History Textbook.* Lanham, Md.: University Press of America, 2000. pp. 137. $45.00 (cloth).

Watras, Joseph. *The Foundations of Educational Curriculum and Diversity: 1556 to the Present.* Boston: Allyn & Bacon, 2001. pp. 416. $51.33 (cloth).

Wechsler, Harold S. *Access to Success in High School: The Middle College Movement.* New York: Teacher's College Press, 2001. pp. 206. $39.00 (cloth).

Whitley, Bernard E., and Patricia Keith-Spiegel. *Academic Dishonesty: An Educator's Guide.* Mahwah, N.J.: Lawrence Erlbaum Associates, Inc., 2002. pp. 169. $17.50 (paper).

BOOKS RECEIVED FALL 2001

Abelson, Robert P. *Statistics as Principled Argument.* Hillsdale, N.J.: Lawrence Erlbaum Associates, Inc., 1995. pp. 221. $32.50 (paper).

Ayers, William. *To Teach: The Journey of a Teacher.* New York: Teachers College Press, 2001. pp. 168. $17.95 (paper).

Banner, James M. Jr., and Harold C. Cannon. *The Elements of Learning.* New Haven, Conn.: Yale University Press, 1999. pp. 182. $11.95 (paper).

Barton, Angela Calabrese, and Margery D. Osborne. *Teaching Science in Diverse: Marginalized Discourses & Classroom Practice.* New York: Peter Lang, 2001. pp. 384. $35.95 (paper).

Bizar, Marilyn, and Rebecca Barr. *School Leadership in Times of Urban Reform*. Mahwah, N.J.: Lawrence Erlbaum Associates, Inc., 2001. pp. 269. $29.95 (paper).

Brewer, Dominic J, Susan M. Gates, and Charles A. Goldman. *In Pursuit of Prestige: Strategy and Competition in U.S. Higher Education*. New Brunswick, N.J.: Transaction, 2002. pp. 175. $29.95 (cloth).

Burstyn, Joan N., Geoff Bender, Ronnie Cassella, Howard W. Gordon, Domingo P. Guerra, Kristen V. Luschen, Rebbeca Stevens, and Kimberly M. Williams. *Preventing Violence in Schools: A Chalenge to American Democracy*. Mahwah, N.J.: Lawrence Erlbaum Associates, Inc., 2001. pp. 249. $89.95 (cloth), $27.50 (paper).

de Carvalho, Maria Eulina P. *Rethinking Family-School Relations: A Critique of Parental Involvement in Schooling*. Mahwah, N.J.: Lawrence Erlbaum Associates, Inc., 2001. pp. 164. $34.50 (cloth), $18.50 (paper).

Deering, Thomas E. *Essays in History and Philosphy of Education*. Dubuque, Iowa: Kendall/ Hunt Publishing, 2001. pp. 208. Price NA.

Deering, Thomas E. *Issues in Teacher Education*. Dubuque, Iowa: Kendall/ Hunt Publishing, 2001. pp. 234. $28.99 (paper).

Fullan, Michael. *The New Meaning of Educational Change*. New York: Teachers College Press, 2001. pp. 312. $54.00 (cloth), $26.95 (paper).

Giroux, Henry A. *Theory and Resistance in Education: Towards a Pedagogy for the Opposition*. Westport, Conn.: Bergin & Garvey, 2001. pp. 320. $24.00 (paper).

Götz, Ignacio L. *Technology and the Spirit*. Westport, Conn.: Praeger, 2001. pp.160. $53.00 (cloth).

Grant, Carl A., and Joy L. Lei. *Global Constructions of Multicultural Education: Theories and Realities*. Mahwah, N.J.: Lawrence Erlbaum Associates, Inc., 2001. pp. 393. $89.95 (cloth), $36.00 (paper).

Graves, Karen, Timothy Glander, and Christine Shea. *Inexcusable Omissions: Clarence Karier and the Critical Tradition in History of Education Scholarship*. New York: Peter Lang, 2001. pp. 313. $29.95 (paper).

Ibarra, Robert A. *Beyond Affirmative Action: Reframing the Context of Higher Education*. Madison: The University of Wisconsin Press, 2001. Pp. 323. $24.95 (paper), $59.95 (cloth).

Ikeda, Daisaku. *SOKA Education: A Buddhist Vision for Teachers, Students and Parents*. Santa Monica, Calif.: Middleway Press, 2001. pp. 208. $25.95 (cloth).

Joseph, Pamela Bolotin, and Gail E. Burnaford. *Images of Schoolteachers in America*. Mahwah, N.J.: Lawrence Erlbaum Associates, Inc., 2001. pp. 260. $27.50 (paper).

Katz, Michael B. *The Irony of Early School Reform: Educational Innovation in Mid-Nineteenth Century Massachusetts.* New York: Teachers College Press, 2001. pp. 368. $44.00 (cloth), $19.95 (paper).

Luke, Carmen. *Globalization and Women in Academia: North/West-South/East.* Mahwah, N.J.: Lawrence Erlbaum Associates, Inc., 2001. pp.267. $74.95 (cloth), $29.95 (paper).

Maher, Frances A., and Janie Victoria Ward. *Gender and Teaching.* Mahwah,N.J.: Lawrence Erlbaum Associates, Inc., 2002. pp. 136. $17.50 (paper).

Meyer, Heinz-Diester, and William Lowe Boyd. *Education Between States, Markets, and Civil Society: Comparative Perspectives.* Mahwah, N.J.: Lawrence Erlbaum Associates, Inc., 2001. pp. 250. $45.95 (cloth).

Molnar, Alex. *Giving Kids the Business.* Boulder, Colo.: Westview, 1996. pp. 223. $25.00 (paper).

Newton, Charles A. *Radical Visions: Stringfellow Barr, Scott Buchanan, and Their Efforts on behalf of Education and Politics in the Twentieth Century.* Westport, Conn.: Greenwood, 2001. pp. 248. $59.00 (cloth).

Nieto, Sonia. *Language, Culture, and Teaching: Critical Perspectives for a New Century.* Mahwah, N.J.: Lawrence Erlbaum Associates, Inc., 2002. pp. 295. $29.95 (paper).

O'Reilly, Patricia, Elizabeth M. Penn, and Kathleen deMarrais. *Educating Young Adolescent Girls.* Mahwah, N.J.: Lawrence Erlbaum Associates, Inc., 2001. pp. 274. $29.95 (paper).

Peshkin, Alan. *Permissible Advantage? The Moral Consequences of Elite Schooling.* Mahwah, N.J.: Lawrence Erlbaum Associates, Inc., 2001. pp. 135. $39.95 (cloth), $16.50 (paper).

Roberts, Shelley. *Remaining and Becoming: Cultural Crosscurrents in an Hispano School.* Mahwah, N.J.: Lawrence Erlbaum Associates, Inc., 2001. pp. 160. $39.95 (cloth), $17.50 (paper).

Schoem, David, and Sylvia Hurtado. *Intergroup Dialogue: Deliberative Democracy in School, College, Community, and Workplace.* Ann Arbor: University of Michigan Press, 2001. pp. 363. $19.95 (paper).

Seller, Maxine Schwartz. *We Built Up Our Lives: Education and Community among Jewish Refugees Interned by Britain in World War II.* Westport, Conn.: Greenwood, 2001. pp. 272. $64.00 (cloth).

Shapiro, Joan Poliner, and Jacqueline A. Stefkovich. *Ethical Leadership and Decision Making in Education: Applying Theoretical Perspectives to Complex Dilemmas.* Mahwah, N.J.: Lawrence Erlbaum Associates, Inc., 2001. pp. 127. $17.50 (paper).

Simon, Katherine G. *Moral Questions in the Classroom: How to Get Kids to Think Deeply About Real Life and Their Schoolwork.* New Haven, Conn.: Yale University Press, 2001. pp. 320. $26.00 (cloth).

Skutnabb-Kangas, Tove. *Linguistic Genocide in Education—Or Worldwide Diversity and Human Rights?* Mahwah, N.J.: Lawrence Erlbaum Associates, Inc., 2000. pp. 785. $55.00 (paper).

Smyth, John. *Critical Politics of Teachers' Work: An Australian Perspective.* New York: Peter Lang, 2001. pp. 320. $29.95 (paper).

Soder, Roger. *The Language of Leadership.* San Francisco: Jossey-Bass, 2001. pp. 211. $28.00 (cloth).

Spring, Joel. *Globalization and Educational Rights: An Intercivilizational Analysis.* Mahwah, N.J.: Lawrence Erlbaum Associates, Inc., 2001. pp. 188. $49.95 (cloth); $19.95 (paper).

Spring, Joel. *Political Agendas for Education: From the Christian Coalition to the Green Party.* Mahwah, N.J.: Lawrence Erlbaum Associates, Inc., 1997. pp. 129. $49.95 (cloth), $17.50 (paper).

Spring, Joel. *The Universal Right to Education: Justification, Definition, and Guidelines.* Mahwah, N.J.: Lawrence Erlbaum Associates, Inc., 2000. pp. 191. $45.50 (cloth), $19.95 (paper).

BOOKS RECEIVED SUMMER 2001

Appleman, Deborah. *Critical Encounters in High School English: Teaching Literary Theory to Adolescents.* New York: Teachers College Press, 2000. pp. 216. $44.00 (cloth), $19.95 (paper).

Bodilly, Susan. *New American Schools' Concept of the Break the Mold Designs: How Designs Evolved and Why.* Santa Monica, Calif.: Rand, 2001. pp. 139. $15.00 (paper).

Callejo-Perez, David M. *Southern Hospitality: Identity, Schools, and the Civil Rights Movement in Mississippi 1964–1972.* New York: Peter Lang, 2001. pp. 176. $24.95 (paper).

Ferguson, Ronald J. *We Know Who We Are: A History of the Blind in Challenging Educational and Socially Constructed Policies (A Study in Policy Archeology).* San Francisco: Caddo Gap Press, 2001. pp. 223. $24.95 (paper).

Keyser, Elizabeth L., and Julie Pfeiffer. *Children's Literature, 29.* New Haven, Conn.: Yale University Press, 2001. pp. 306. $45.00 (cloth), $19.00 (paper).

Kinsler, Kimberly, and Mae Gamble. *Reforming Schools.* New York: Continuum, 2001. pp. 256. $89.95 (cloth), $29.95 (paper).

Levin, Henry M. *Privatizing Education: Can the Marketplace Deliver Choice, Efficiency, Equity, and Social Cohesion?* Cambridge, Mass.: Westview, 2001. pp. 373. $35.00 (paper).

Lindsay, Beverly, and Manuel J. Justiz. *The Quest for Equity in Higher Education: Toward New Paradigms in an Evolving Affirmative Action Era.* Albany: State University of New York Press, 2001. pp. 319. $71.50 (cloth), $23.95 (paper).

McNally, John. *The Student Body.* Madison: The University of Wisconsin Press, 2001. pp. 280. $16.95 (paper).

Nucci, Larry P. *Education in the Moral Domain.* New York: Cambridge University Press, 2001. pp. 242. $54.95 (cloth); $19.95 (paper).

Pinar, William F. *The Gender of Racial Politics and Violence: Lynching, Prison Rape, and the Crisis of Masculinity.* New York: Peter Lang, 2001. pp. 1280. $55.95 (paper).

Riemer, Frances Julia. *Working at the Margins: Moving off Welfare in America.* Albany: State University of New York Press, 2001. pp. 297. $22.95 (paper).

Ward, Angela, and Rita Bouvier. *Resting Lightly on Mother Earth: The Aboriginal Experience in Urban Educational Settings.* Calgary, Alberta, Canada: Detselig Enterprises Ltd., 2001. pp. 195. Price NA (paper).

Watras, Joseph. *The Foundations of Educational Curriculum and Diversity: 1565 to the Present.* Boston: Allyn & Bacon, 2002. pp. 416. $51.33 (cloth).

Wilson, Anna Victoria, and William E. Segall. *Oh, Do I Remember!: Experiences of Teachers During the Desegregation of Austin's Schools, 1964–1971.* Albany: State University of New York Press, 2001. pp.186. $19.95 (paper).

Witte, John F. *An Analysis of America's First Voucher Program.* Princeton, N.J.: Princeton University Press, 2001. pp. 221. $40.00 (cloth), $18.95 (paper).

BOOKS RECEIVED SPRING 2001

Aronson, Rosa. *At-Risk Students Defy the Odds: Overcoming Barriers to Educational Success.* Lanham, Md.: Scarecrow Press, 2001. pp. 144. $45.00 (cloth), $19.95 (paper).

Ayers, William, Bernardine Dohrn, and Rick Ayers. *Zero Tolerance: Resisting the Drive for Punishment in our Schools.* New York: The New Press, 2001. pp. 266. $17.95 (paper).

Barone, Tom. *Touching Eternity: The Enduring Outcomes of Teaching.* New York: Teachers College Press, 2001. pp. 208. $50.00 (cloth), $22.95 (paper).

Berlak, Ann, and Sekani Moyenda. *Taking it Personally: Racism in the Classroom from Kindergarten to College.* Philadelphia: Temple University Press. 2001. pp. 216. $59.50 (cloth), $19.95 (paper).

Birnbaum, Shira. *Law and Order and School: Daily Life in an Educational Program for Juvenile Delinquents.* Philadelphia: Temple University Press, 2001. pp. 208. $59.50 (cloth), $18.95 (paper).

Clark, Christopher M. *Talking Shop: Authentic Conversation and Teacher Learning.* New York: Teachers College Press, 2001. pp. 208. $48.00 (cloth), $22.95 (paper).

Duckworth, Eleanor. *"Tell Me More": Listening to Learners Explain.* New York: Teachers College Press, 2001. pp. 216. $44.00 (cloth), $19.95 (paper).

Gallego, Margaret A., and Sandra Hollingsworth. *What Counts as Literacy: Challenging the School Standard.* New York: Teachers College Press, 2000. pp. 325. $62.00 (cloth), $29.95 (paper).

Goodheart, Eugene. *Culture and the Radical Conscience.* New Brunswick, N.J.: Transaction, 2001. pp. 192. $24.95 (paper).

Hansen, David T. *Exploring the Moral Heart of Teaching: Toward a Teacher's Creed.* New York: Teachers College Press, 2001. pp. 240. $46.00 (cloth); $21.95 (paper).

Kingston-Mann, Esther, and Tim Sieber. *Achieving Against the Odds: How Academics Become Teachers of Diverse Students.* Philadelphia: Temple University Press, 2001. pp. 240. $59.50 (cloth), $19.95 (paper).

Lieberman, Ann, and Lynne Miller. *Teachers Caught in the Action: Professional Development That Matters.* New York: Teachers College Press, 2001. pp. 256. $53.00 (cloth), $23.95 (paper).

Portelli, John P., and R. Patrick Solomon. *The Erosion of Democracy in Education: From Critique to Possibilities.* Calgary, Alberta, Canada: Detselig Enterprises Ltd. 2001. Pp. 328. $26.95 (paper).

Simon, Christopher A. *To Run a School: Administrative Organization and Learning.* Westport, Conn.: Praeger, 2001. pp. 200. $55.00 (cloth).

Vedder, Richard K. *Can Teachers Own Their Own Schools?* Oakland, Calif.: The Independent Institute, 2000. pp. 57. $12.95 (paper).

Warner, Dorothy, and William D. Guthrie. *Knowing Good Schools: A Guide to Rating Public High Schools.* Westport, Conn.: Bergin & Garvey, 2001. pp. 176. $55.00 (cloth).

Wineburg, Sam. *Historical Thinking and Other Unnatural Acts: Charting the Future of Teaching the Past.* Philadelphia: Temple University Press, 2001. pp. 272. $69.50 (cloth), $22.95 (paper).

York, Neil L. *Fiction as Fact: "The Horse Soldiers" and Popular Memory.* Kent, Ohio: The Kent State University Press, 2001. pp. 179. $28.00 (cloth), $18.00 (paper).

BOOKS RECEIVED WINTER 2001

Arguelles, Antonio, and Andrew Gonczi. *Competency Based Education and Training: A World Perspective.* Mexico: Noriega Editores, 2000. pp. 229. Price NA (paper).

Beyer, Landon B. *The Arts, Popular Culture, and Social Change.* New York: Peter Lang, 2000. pp. 157. $24.95 (paper).

Bray, Mark. *Double-Shift Schooling: Design and Operation for Cost Effectiveness.* Paris: UNESCO, 2000. pp. 92. $15.00 (paper).

Brindley, Thomas A. *The China Youth Corps in Taiwan.* New York: Peter Lang, 1999. pp. 155. $38.95 (cloth).

Burnaford, Gail, Joseph Fischer, and David Hobson. *Teachers Doing Research: The Power of Action Through Inquiry.* Mahwah, N.J.: Lawrence Erlbaum Associates, Inc., 2001. pp. 389. $27.50 (paper).

Coleman, Geraldine. *Issues in Education: View from the Other Side of the Room.* Westport, Conn.: Bergin & Garvey, 2001. pp. 206. $55.00 (cloth).

Daugherty, Richard F. *Special Education: A Summary of Legal Requirements, Terms, and Trends.* Westport, Conn.: Bergin & Garvey, 2001. pp. 184. $49.95 (cloth).

Fischman, Gustavo E. *Imagining Teachers: Rethinking Gender Dynamics in the Classroom.* Lanham, Md.: Rowman & Littlefield, 2000. pp. 211. $80.00 (cloth), $26.95 (paper).

Gilman, Sander L. *The Fortunes of the Humanities: Thoughts for After the Year 2000.* Stanford, Calif.: Stanford University Press, 2000. pp. 127. $14.95 (paper).

Gorski, Paul C. *Multicultural Education and the Internet: Intersections and Integrations.* Boston: McGraw-Hill Higher Education, 2001. pp. 162. Price NA (paper).

Hall, Julia. *Canal Town Youth: Community Organization and the Development of Adolescent Identity.* Albany: State University of New York Press, 2001. pp. 163. $18.05 (paper).

Hart, Tobin. *From Information to Transformation: Education for the Evolutions of Consciousness.* New York: Peter Lang, 2001. pp. 196. $29.95 (paper).

Jacobs, Travis Beal. *Eisenhower at Columbia.* New Brunswick, N.J.: Transaction, 2001. pp. 354. $39.95 (cloth).

Jipson, Janice A., and Richard T. Johnson. *Resistance and Representation: Rethinking Childhood Education.* New York: Peter Lang, 2001. pp. 368. $32.95 (paper).

Kelly, Michael J. *Planning for Education in the Context of HIV/AIDS.* Paris: UNESCO, 2000. pp. 108. Price NA (paper).

Martusewicz, Rebecca A. *Seeking Passage: Post-Structuralism, Pedagogy, Ethics.* New York: Teachers College Press, 2001. pp. 143. $52.00 (cloth), $24.95 (paper).

McCormick, Virginia E. *Educational Architecture in Ohio: From One-Room Schools and Carnegie Libraries to Community Education Villages.* Kent, Ohio: Kent State University Press, 2001. pp. 318. $45.00 (cloth).

Norwich, Brahm. *Education and Psychology in Interaction: Working with Uncertainty in Interconnected Fields.* New York: Routledge, 2000. pp. 259. $90.00 (cloth).

Outcalt, Charles L., Shannon K. Farris, and Kathleen N. McMahon. *Developing Non-Hierarchical Leadership on Campus: Case Studies and Practices in Higher Education.* Westport, Conn.: Greenwood, 2001. pp. 280. $65.00 (cloth).

Ovando, Carlos J., and Peter McClaren. *The Politics of Multiculturalism and Bilingual Education: Students and Teachers Caught in the Cross Fire.* Boston: McGraw-Hill Higher Education, 2000. pp. 240. $34.80 (paper).

Paludi, Michele A. *Human Development in Multicultural Contexts: A Book of Readings.* Upper Saddle River, N.J.: Prentice Hall, 2001. pp. 270. $30.67 (paper).

Peters, Michael, James Marshall, and Paul Smeyers. *Nietzsche's Legacy for Education: Past and Present Values.* Westport, Conn.: Bergin & Garvey, 2001. pp. 264. $65.00 (cloth).

Scales. T. Laine. *All That Fits a Woman: Training Southern Baptist Women for Charity and Mission, 1907–1926.* Macon, GA: Mercer University Press, 2000. pp. 287. $30.00 (cloth).

Scheerens, Jaap. *Improving School Effectiveness.* Paris: UNESCO, 2000. pp. 137. Price NA (paper).

Schultz, Fred. *Annual Editions: Multicultural Education.* Guilford, Conn.: McGraw-Hill/Dushkin, 2001. pp. 227. $19.90 (paper).

Smith, Stacy. *The Democratic Potential of Charter Schools.* New York: Peter Lang, 2001. pp. 304. $32.95 (paper).

Spring, Joel. *Deculturalization and the Struggle for Equality: A Brief History of the Education of Dominated Cultures in the United States.* Boston: McGraw-Hill Higher Education, 2001. pp. 125. $23.80 (paper).

Titone, Connie, and Karen E. Maloney. *Women's Philosophies of Education: Thinking Through Our Mothers.* Upper Saddle River, N.J.: Merrill, Prentice Hall, 1999. pp. 214. $35.00 (paper).

Valencia, Richard R., and Lisa A. Suzuki. *Intelligence Testing and Minority Students: Foundations, Performance Factors, and Assessment Issues.* Thousand Oaks, Calif.: Sage, 2001. pp. 388. $74.95 (cloth).

Weber, Lynn. *Understanding Race, Class, Gender, and Sexuality: A Conceptual Framework.* Boston: McGraw-Hill Higher Education, 2001. pp. 224. $34.10 (paper).

Weikart, David P. *Early Childhood Education: Need and Opportunity.* Paris: UNESCO, 2000. pp. 93. Price NA (paper).

Wilson, Bruce L., and H. Dickson Corbett. *Listening to Urban Kids: School Reform and the Teachers They Want.* Albany: State University of New York Press, 2001. pp. 144. $16.95 (paper).

BOOKS RECEIVED WINTER 2000

Armstrong, David G., Kenneth T. Henson, and Tom V. Savage. *Teaching Today: An Introduction to Education.* Upper Saddle River, N.J.: Merrill Prentice Hall, 2001. pp. 471. $40.00 (paper).

Chartock, Roselle K. *Educational Foundations: An Anthology.* Upper Saddle River, N.J.: Merrill Prentice Hall, 2000. pp. 344. $36.00 (paper).

Faltis, Christian J. *Joinfostering: Teaching and Learning in Multilingual Classrooms,* 3rd ed. Upper Saddle River, N.J.: Merrill Prentice Hall, 2001. pp. 203. $35.00 (paper).

Gotz, Ignacio L. *Manners and Violence.* Westport, Conn.: Praeger, 2000. pp. 152. $52.50 (cloth).

Grant, Carl A., and Mary Louise Gomez. *Campus and Classroom: Making Schooling Multicultural,* 2nd ed. Upper Saddle River, N.J.: Merrill Prentice Hall, 2001. pp. 375. $39.00 (paper).

Gutek, Gerald L. *Historical and Philosophical Foundations of Education: A Biographical Introduction,* 3rd ed. Upper Saddle River, N.J.: Merrill Prentice Hall, 2001. pp. 225. $42.00 (paper).

Gutek, Gerald L. *Historical and Philosophical Foundations of Education: Selected Readings.* Upper Saddle River, N.J.: Merrill Prentice Hall, 2001. pp. 225. $42.00 (paper).

Hernandez, Hilda. *Multicultural Education: A Teacher's Guide to Linking Context, Process, and Content,* 2nd ed. Upper Saddle River, N.J.: Merrill Prentice Hall, 2001. pp. 344. $52.00 (paper).

Jacobsen, David Andrew. *Philosophy in Classroom Teaching: Bridging the Gap.* Upper Saddle River, N.J.: Merrill Prentice Hall, 1999. pp. 283. $46.00 (paper).

kiluva-ndunda, mutindi mumbua. *Women's Agency and Educational Policy: The Experiences of the Women of Kilome, Kenya.* Albany: State University of New York Press, 2001. pp. 194. $54.50 (paper).

Lebow, Eileen F. *The Bright Boys: The History of Townsend Harris High School.* Westport, Conn.: Greenwood, 2000. pp. 248. $62.50 (cloth).

Lewis, Lionel S. *When Power Corrupts: Academic Governing Boards in the Shadow of the Adelphi Case.* Somerset, N.J.: Transaction, 2000. pp. 195. $34.95 (cloth).

Mitchell, Bruce M., and Robert E. Salsbury. *Multicultural Education in the U.S.: A Guide to Policies and Programs in the 50 States.* Westport, Conn.: Greenwood, 2000. pp. 296. $75.00 (cloth).

Ozmon, Howard A., and Samuel M. Craver. *Philosophical Foundations of Education,* 6th ed. Upper Saddle River, N.J.: Merrill Prentice Hall, 1999. pp. 389. $49.00 (paper).

Pai, Young, and Susan A. Adler. *Cultural Foundations of Education,* 3rd ed. Upper Saddle River, N.J.: Merrill Prentice Hall, 2001. pp. 262. $45.65 (paper).

Pitman, Mary Anne, and Debbie Zorn, eds. *Caring as Tenacity: Stories of Urban School Survival.* Cresskill, N.J.: Hampton, 2000. pp. 141. $42.50 (paper).

Preskill, Stephen L., and Robin Smith Jacobvitz. *Stories of Teaching: A Foundation for Educational Renewal.* Upper Saddle River, N.J.: Merrill Prentice Hall, 2001. pp. 211. $28.00 (paper).

Pulliam, John D., and James J. Van Patten. *History of Education in America,* 7th ed. Upper Saddle River, N.J.: Merrill Prentice Hall, 1999. pp. 334. $43.00 (paper).

Siskind, Theresa Gayle. *Cases for Middle School Educators.* Lanham, Md.: Scarecrow Education, 2000. pp. 176. $36.50 (cloth).

Strouse, Joan H. *Exploring Socio-Cultural Themes in Education: Readings in Social Foundations,* 2nd ed. Upper Saddle River, N.J.: Merrill Prentice Hall, 2001. pp. 345. $41.00 (paper).

Urban, Wayne J. *Gender, Race, and the National Education Association: Professionalism and its Limitations.* New York: Routledge Falmer, 2000. pp. 300. $42.00 (paper).

Wallen, Norman E., and Jack R. Fraenkel. *Educational Research: A Guide to the Process,* 2nd ed. Mahwah, N.J.: Lawrence Erlbaum Associates, Inc., 2000. pp. 550. $55.00 (paper).

Webb L. Dean, Arlene Metha, and K. Forbis Jordan. *Foundations of American Education,* 3rd ed. Upper Saddle River, N.J.: Merrill Prentice Hall, 2000. pp. 599. $60.00 (paper).

BOOKS RECEIVED FALL 2000

Allison, Clinton B., ed. *Kellie McGarrh's Hangin' in Tough: Mildred E. Doyle, School Superintendent.* New York: Peter Lang, 2000. pp. 160. $29.95 (paper).

Armitage, Peter B. *Political Relationship and Narrative Knowledge: A Critical Analysis of School Authoritarianism.* Westport, Conn.: Greenwood, 2000. pp. 256. $59.95 (cloth).

Banks, James A., and Cherry A McGee Banks, eds. *Multicultural Education: Issues and Perspectives,* 4th ed. New York: Wiley, 2001. pp. 441. $61.00 (paper).

Burch, Kerry T. *Eros and the Education Principle of Democracy.* New York: Peter Lang, 2000. pp. 240. $29.95 (paper).

Butche, Robert W. *Image of Excellence: The Ohio University School.* New York: Peter Lang, 2000. pp. 407. $32.95 (paper).

Carnoy, Martin. *Globalization and Educational Reform: What Planners Need to Know.* Paris: UNESCO, 2000. pp. 95. $15.00 (paper).

Cuban, Larry, and Dorothy Shipps, eds. *Reconstructing the Common Good in Education: Coping With Intractable American Dilemmas.* Stanford, Calif.: Stanford University Press, 2000. pp. 283. $55.00 (cloth), $19.95 (paper).

Finnan, Christine, and Julie D. Swanson. *Accelerating the Learning of All Students: Cultivating Culture Change in Schools, Classrooms, and Individuals.* Boulder, Colo.: Westview, 2000. pp. 190. $22.00 (paper).

Frase, Larry E., and William Streshly. *Top 10 Myths in Education: Fantasies Americans Love to Believe.* Lanham, Md.: Scarecrow Education, 2000. pp. 144. $14.95 (paper).

Ginsberg, Margery B., and Raymond J. Wlodkowski. *Creating Highly Motivating Classrooms for all Students: A School Wide Approach to Powerful Teaching with Diverse Learners.* San Francisco: Jossey-Bass, 2000. pp. 305. $29.95 (cloth).

Grote, John E. *Paideia Agonistes: The Lost Soul of Modern Education.* Lanham, Md.: University Press of America, 2000. pp. 332. $32.50 (paper).

Kelly, M. Deirdre. *Pregnant with Meaning: Teen Mothers and the Politics of Inclusive Schooling.* New York: Peter Lang, 2000. pp. 272. $29.95 (paper).

McGinn, N., and T. Welsh. *Decentralization of Education: Why, When, What, and How?* Paris: UNESCO, 2000. pp. 95. $15.00 (paper).

Mitchell, Bruce M., and Robert E. Salsbury. *Multicultural Education in the U.S.: A Guide to Policies and Programs in the 50 States*. Westport, Conn.: Greenwood, 2000. pp. 296. $65.00 (cloth).

O'Grady, Carolyn R., ed. *Integrating Service Learning and Multicultural Education in Colleges and Universities*. Mahwah, N.J.: Lawrence Erlbaum Associates, Inc., 2000. pp. 300. $69.95 (cloth), $34.50 (paper).

Owen, Jane C., and Martha N. Ovando. *Superintendent's Guide to Creating Community*. Lanham, Md.: Scarecrow Education, 2000. pp. 152. $45.00 (cloth), $27.95 (paper).

Sanders, Mavis G., ed. *Schooling Students Placed At Risk: Research, Policy and Practice in the Education of Poor and Minority Adolescents*. Mahwah, N.J.: Lawrence Erlbaum Associates, Inc., 2000. pp. 375. $79.95 (cloth), $39.95 (paper).

Shields, Carolyn M., and Steven Lynn Oberg. *Year-round Schooling: Promises and Pitfalls*. Lanham, Md.: Scarecrow Education, 2000. pp. 280. $45.00 (cloth).

Shorris, Earl. *Riches for the Poor: The Clemente Course in the Humanities*. New York: Norton, 2000. pp. 273. $13.45 (paper).

Short, Paula M., and Jay Paredes Scribner. *Case Studies of the Superintendency*. Lanham, Md.: Scarecrow Education, 2000. pp. 176. $29.00 (cloth).

Swing, Elizabeth Sherman, Jurgen Schriewer, and Francois Orivel, eds. *Problems and Prospects in European Education*. Westport, Conn.: Greenwood, 2000. pp. 296. $75.00 (cloth).

BOOKS RECEIVED SUMMER 2000

Aby, Stephen H., and James C. Kuhn. *Academic Freedom: A guide to the Literature*. Westport, Conn.: Greenwood, 2000. pp. 240. $75.00 (cloth).

Brown, Richard Harvey, and J. Daniel Schubert, eds. *Knowledge and Power in Higher Education*. New York: Teachers College Press, 2000. pp. 200. $56.00 (cloth).

Curry, Barbara K. *Women in Power: Pathways to Leadership in Education*. Forward by Maxine Greene. New York: Teachers College Press, 2000. pp. 128. $44.00 (cloth), $21.95 (paper).

Fletcher, Scott. *Education and Emancipation: Theory and Practice in a New Constellation*. New York: Teachers College Press, 2000. pp. 207. $50.00 (cloth), $23.95 (paper).

Jones, Bruce Anthony, ed. *Educational Leadership: Policy Dimensions in the 21st Century*. Stamford, Conn.: Ablex, 2000. pp. 170. $58.50 (cloth), $29.95 (paper).

Koblik, Steven, and Stephen R. Graubard. *Distinctively American: The Residential Liberal Arts Colleges.* Somerset, N.J.: Transaction, 2000. pp. 315. $29.95 (paper).

Lyman, Linda L. *How Do They Know You Care: The Principal's Challenge.* Foreword by Roland S. Barth. New York: Teachers College Press, 2000. pp. 160. $21.95 (paper).

Menck, Peter. *Looking into Classrooms: Papers on Didactics.* Stamford, Conn.: JAI/Ablex, 2000. pp. 143. $73.25 (cloth), $32.50 (paper).

Miller-Bernal, Leslie. *Separate by Degree: Women Students' Experiences in Single-Sex and Coeducational Colleges.* New York: Peter Lang, 2000. pp. 375. $29.95 (paper).

O'Hair, Mary John, H. James McLaughlin, and Ulrich C. Reitzug. *Foundations of Democratic Education.* Orlando, Fla.: Harcourt College Publishers, 2000. pp. 544. $76.95 (cloth).

Pollard, Diane S., and Cheryl S. Ajirotutu, eds. *African-Centered Schooling in Theory and Practice.* Westport, Conn.: Greenwood, 1999. pp. 240. $65.00 (cloth).

Thomas, Cornell, Paullete Fitzhugh-Walker, and Phildra T. Jefferies. *We Can Have Better Schools.* San Francisco: Caddo Gap Press, 2000. pp. 132. $19.95 (paper).

Ravitch, Diane, and Joseph P. Viteritti, eds. *Lessons from New York: City Schools.* Baltimore: Johns Hopkins University Press, 2000. pp. 405. $59.95 (cloth), $21.50 (paper).

Roberts, Peter. *Education, Literacy, and Humanization: Exploring the Work of Paulo Freire.* Critical Studies in Education Series, Henry Giroux, ed. Westport, Conn.: Greenwood, 2000. pp. 192. $59.95 (cloth).

Sattler, Cheryl L. *Teaching to Transcend.* Albany: State University of New York Press, 2000. pp. 150. $15.95 (paper).

Wilson, Mark, and George Engelhard, Jr., eds. *Objective Measurement: Theory into Practice, Volume 5.* Stamford, Conn.: Ablex, 2000. pp. 320. $78.50 (cloth), $39.95 (paper).

Wisniewski, Richard, ed. *Reforming a College: The University of Tennessee Story.* New York: Peter Lang, 2000. pp. 216. $29.95 (paper).

BOOKS RECEIVED SPRING 2000

Abu-Duhou, Ibtisam. *School-Based Management.* Paris: UNESCO: 1999. pp. 97. $15.00 (paper).

Apple, Michael. *Official Knowledge: Democratic Education in a Conservative Age,* 2nd ed. New York: Routledge, 2000. pp. 220. $20.99 (paper).

Berube, Maurice R. *Eminent Educators: Studies in Intellectual Influence*. Westport, Conn.: Greenwood, 1999. pp. 192. $ 57.95 (cloth).

Bray, Mark. *The Shadow Education System: Private Tutoring and its Implications for Planners*. Paris: International Institute for International Planning and the United Nations, 1999. pp. 97. $15.00 (paper).

Duarte, Eduardo Manuel, and Stacy Smith. *Foundational Perspectives in Multicultural Education*. New York: Longman, 2000. pp. 360. $54.00 (paper).

Forcey, Linda Rennie, and Ian M. Harris, eds. *Peacebuilding for Adolescents: Strategies for Educators and Community Leaders*. New York: Peter Lang, 1999. pp. 376. $32.95 (paper).

Glander, Timothy. *Origins of Mass Communications Research During the American Cold War: Educational Effects and Contemporary Implications*. Mahwah, N.J.: Lawrence Erlbaum Associates, Inc., 2000. pp. 191. $29.95 (paper).

Glanz, Jeffery, and Linda S. Behar-Horenstein, eds. *Paradigm Debates in Curriculum and Supervision: Modern and Postmodern Perspectives*. Westport, Conn.: Greenwood, 2000. pp. 312. $65.00 (cloth).

Gutek, Gerald L. *American Education 1945–2000*. Prospect Heights, Ill.: Waveland, 2000. pp. 343. $22.95 (paper).

Hill, Clifford, and Eric Larsen. *Children and Reading Tests*. Stamford, Conn.: Ablex, 2000. pp. 425. $73.25 (cloth), $39.50 (paper).

Joseph, Pamela Bolotin, Stephanie Luster Bravmann, Mark A. Windschitl, Edward R. Mikel, and Nancy Stewart Green. *Cultures of Curriculum*. Mahwah, N.J.: Lawrence Erlbaum Associates, Inc., 2000. pp. 191. $22.50 (paper).

Kaplan, Jeffery S., ed. *Identity Issues: Using Literature to Help Troubled Teenagers*. Westport, Conn.: Greenwood, 1999. pp. 248. $39.95 (cloth).

Kennedy, Rosa L., and Jerome H. Morton. *A School for Healing: Alternative Strategies for Teaching At-Risk Students*. New York: Peter Lang, 1999. pp. 200. $29.95 (cloth).

Klieberd, Herbert M. *Schooled to Work: Vocationalism and the American Curriculum 1876–1946*. New York: Teachers College Press, 2000. pp. 278. $22.95 (paper).

Manegold, Catherine S. *In Glory's Shadow: Shannon Faulkner, the Citadel, and a Changing America*. New York: Knopf, 2000. pp. 330. $26.95 (cloth).

Mazurek, Kas, Margaret A. Winzer, and Czeslaw Majorek. *Education in a Global Society: A Comparative Perspective*. Needham Heights, Mass.: Allyn & Bacon, 2000. pp. 419. $62.00 (cloth).

Noel, Jana. *Developing Multicultural Educators.* New York: Longman, 2000. pp. 190. $40.33 (paper).

Noel, Jana. *Sources: Notable Selections in Multicultural Education.* Guilford, Conn.: McGraw-Hill/Dushkin, 2000. pp. 318. $16.75 (paper).

Popp, Jerome A. *Cognitive Science and Philosophy of Education: Toward a Unified Theory of Learning and Teaching.* San Francisco: Caddo Gap Press, 1999. pp. 240. $24.95 (paper).

Portales, Marco. *Crowding Out Latinos: Mexican Americans in the Public Schools.* Philadelphia: Temple University Press, 2000. pp. 208. $19.95 (paper).

Riding, Richard J., and Stephen G. Rayner, eds. *International Perspectives on Individual Differences: Volume I, Cognitive Styles.* Stamford, Conn.: Ablex, 2000. pp. 392. $42.50 (paper).

Schoenbach, Ruth, Cynthia Greenleaf, Christina Cziko, and Lori Hurwitz. *Reading for Understanding: A Guide to Improving Reading in Middle and High School Classrooms.* San Francisco: Jossey-Bass, 1999. pp. 190. $19.95 (paper).

Spigelman, Candace. *Across Property Lines: Textual Ownership in Writing Groups.* Carbondale: Southern Illinois University Press, 2000. pp. 177. $14.95 (paper).

Spring, Joel. *Education and the Rise of the Global Economy.* Mahwah, N.J.: Lawrence Erlbaum Associates, Inc., 1998. pp. 234. $24.95 (paper).

Steet, Linda. *Veils and Daggers.* Philadelphia: Temple University Press, 2000. pp. 208. $21.95 (paper).

Widen, Marvin, and Paulette Lemma, eds. *Ground Level Reform in Teacher Education: Changing Schools of Education.* Bellingham, Wash.: Temeron Books Inc., 1999. pp. 232. $22.95 (paper).

Winkler, Barbara Scott, and Carolyn DiPalma, eds. *Teaching Introduction to Women's Studies: Expectations and Strategies.* Westport, Conn.: Greenwood, 1999. pp. 288. $59.95 (cloth).

STILL AVAILABLE FOR REVIEW

Gabbard, David A., ed. *Knowledge and Power in the Global Economy: Politics and the Rhetoric of School Reform.* Mahwah, N.J.: Lawrence Erlbaum Associates, Inc., 2000. pp. 430. $39.95 (paper).

Lipkin, Arthur. *Understanding Homosexuality, Changing Schools: A Text for Teachers, Counselors, and Administrators.* Boulder, Colo.: Westview, 1999. pp. 483. $69.00 (cloth).

Olessen, Mark. *Michel Foucault: Materialism and Education.* Westport, Conn.: Greenwood, 1999. pp. 216. $59.95 (cloth).

Ovando, Carlos J., and Peter McLaren. *Multiculturalism and Bilingual Education: Students and Teachers Caught in the Cross Fire.* New York: McGraw-Hill, 1999. pp. 235. $32.70 (paper).

Peter, Michael, ed. *After the Disciplines: The Emergence of Cultural Studies.* Westport, Conn.: Greenwood, 1999. pp. 300. $69.50 (cloth).

Pinar, William F., ed. *Contemporary Curriculum Discourse.* New York: Peter Lang, 1999. pp. 608. $39.95 (paper).

Rousmaniere, Kate, Ian Grosvenor, and Martin Lawn, eds. *Silence and Images: The Social History of the Classroom.* New York: Peter Lang, 1999. pp. 288. $29.95 (paper).

www.ingramcontent.com/pod-product-compliance
Ingram Content Group UK Ltd.
Pitfield, Milton Keynes, MK11 3LW, UK
UKHW041840280225
455677UK00010B/259